Feeding Your Horse and Pony

Diana R. Tuke

J. A. Allen

London

British Library Cataloguing in Publication Data
Tuke, Diana R.
1. Horses – Feeding and feeds
I. Title
636.1'0852   SF285.5

ISBN 0–85131–456–2

Published in Great Britain by
J. A. Allen & Company Limited,
1, Lower Grosvenor Place, Buckingham Palace Road,
London, SW1W 0EL
First published 1988
Reprinted 1993

Printed and bound in Great Britain by WBC, Bridgend, Mid Glam.

Contents

List of Illustrations

Preface

Almost a decade has passed since I wrote FEEDING YOUR HORSE, and although the basic concepts of feeding have hardly changed, there have been innovations such as the micronising of cereals, *Horsehage* and herbal products which I have now included to give a comprehensive and completely up-to-date study of Equine Feeding.

Several other books have been published on feeding in recent years, but many are very technical, and my aim is, as it was with the first edition, to give owners of horses and ponies a sound, practical insight into feeding, without blinding them with too much high-powered science.

As well as being revised and updated, this new edition has an extended introduction which gives the origins of our native breeds of ponies and horses, so as to help us adjust their feeding to their particular needs. The hardback, wipeable cover is a practical improvement for a book whose rightful place is in the feed-room!

Although *Feeding Your Horse* included ponies, the new title makes it clear that ponies are included in this edition, and I would like to assure all owners of horses and ponies, whatever they are used for, that *Feeding Your Horse and Pony* was written for each and every one of them.

D.R.T. 1988.

1 Principles of Sound Feeding

To understand feeding it is essential to know something of the origin of our horses and ponies and the type of climate and terrain they are used to in their native environment. Our native breeds – who provide either the foundation of, or, as pure-breds are, our children's ponies and driving ponies and in many cases our horses too – are noted for their hardiness and ability to live off sparse grazing, providing they have a wide area to roam over. This area, in the form of big rocks and hillsides or glens, will also provide them with shelter from the prevailing weather.

In the very north of Scotland is the tiniest of British ponies – the Shetland. Standing not more than 10·2 hh this short-legged, big bodied pony lives off the salt-laden land around Scotland's foreshores, hence the reason it requires access to more salt than normal when moved away from its native haunts. It must always have a salt lick.

Also from Scotland, especially on the Western Isles and their neighbouring mainland, is the Highland. Its height varies from 12·2 hh on the outer Islands, to 14·2 hh for the heavy mainland ponies; the lighter riding type from the inner islands varies from 13·2 hh to 14·2 hh.

On the bleak hills of the north of England are found the Fell pony, 13·2 hh and the, heavier, Dale pony at some 14·2 hh. The Fell is a ride and drive pony, whereas the Dale is used largely on the land and as a trap pony, though it does get ridden too.

Wales, with its rough mountains and, in winter, harsh climate, provides us with the Welsh pony. This breed is, of course, famous the world over and is, too, the foundation of many of our ponies and horses today, both for riding and driving, besides filling both roles in its pure-bred form. The

1

largest of these ponies are the section D Welsh Cob – 14 hh to 15·1 hh; known as section C is a riding type who is also much used in harness. The very pretty section B is well known in our show rings in the 13·2 hh classes, while, lastly, the Welsh Mountain, section A, pony stands no higher than 12 hh and is a pony both to ride and drive.

In the West of England is the hardy Exmoor pony. Its mares must not exceed 12·2 hh and its stallions 12·3 hh. Also in the West Country is the Dartmoor pony. Exmoor can be bleak in winter, but Dartmoor is even worse and grazing is in short supply. Here too, the ponies only go up to 12·2 hh, being very much a child's riding pony.

Along the south coast of England the New Forest pony can be found, from 12 hh to 14·2 hh. They, too, are born to live off poor grazing and if kept in fields must be watched for rich land is not kind to them – like all the native breeds of Britain they require clean, short grass and room to move about in order to get exercise. Native ponies are excellent at utilising their food, getting far more out of it than their better-, or cross-bred cousins.

In the far west of Ireland, in the county that bears the same name and runs down to the Atlantic, the Connemara pony is the native breed. Its height, up to 14·2 hh – some will grow bigger away from their native land – makes it an excellent children's pony. It is suitable also for small adults and as a trap pony. Crossed with the Thoroughbred the Connemara produces some of the best of our small horses.

So much for our hardy native ponies; but many are not pure-bred, and the most usual crosses are with the Arab horse, whose height ranges from under 14 hh to 15 hh or ever bigger in a few cases. The Arab has a very fine coat unsuited to harsh climates and when crossed with a native pony the density of the coat tends to be reduced, making it necessary to feed the pony more and keep it warmer. However, the Arab is hardy when it comes to food, due to its origin in the desert, and requires feeding more on the lines of a pony than the Thoroughbred. Indeed, the Thoroughbred horse, like the Arab, has a fine skin and coat but, though originating from the Arab many generations ago, now needs top-quality food and plenty of it, plus warmth and shelter. It cannot or should not live out at night in winter. Many

2

of our native breeds are crossed with Thoroughbreds in order to produce a better riding pony or horse. They do retain some hardiness, but must be treated in recognition of their Thoroughbred blood. Nowadays many of the Continental breeds are coming to Britain and being crossed with our horses. To determine how they should be treated it is best to consult their breed societies or other suitable sources for, along with our own Cleveland Bay and the Irish Draught, these Continental breeds are being used to produce our bigger, stronger horses with plenty of bone and substance.

All horses and ponies have a right to be correctly and adequately fed, regardless of how or where they are kept. For some inexplicable reason the intricacies of sound feeding seems to elude many owners. Feeding both horses and ponies is closely related; basically they are the same, merely requiring commonsense to realise that a small pony being ridden by a child *must not* receive the same energy producing foods as a horse or pony being ridden by a more experienced rider. In this book I am concerned with horses as a species – ponies therefore will only be specifically referred to when required, my aim being to dispel some of the mysteries that seem to surround the art of feeding – an art that can be acquired. Semi or total ignorance of this all-important subject can only lead ultimately to the detriment of any horse, whereas the reward that comes from owning or caring for a really fit, healthy horse is very real indeed. There is far more to feeding than just tipping a bucket of food into a manger, or dumping out an armful of hay. Horses are highly individual and therefore must be fed as such, each with their own diet sheet. Without sound feeding no horse can be expected to give of its best; and if inadequately fed, will either become ill, or even die.

Initially one must study a horse's temperament and its conformation, the latter being important, as a narrow frame will never hold the same amount of food as a big one. A narrow-framed horse will require highly nourishing food to maintain condition, whereas a big barrelled one will require bulk to fill it up. Temperament is all-important as a calm horse will make full use of its food intake, while its highly strung counterpart will burn up part of its ration with fretting, and if not fed very carefully will proceed to give its rider a most uncomfortable

3

time! The aim with every horse should be to produce an individual that is fit and alert with a bright eye and a body that carries neither an excess of flesh nor lack of it, but is well covered. Extremes either way are to the detriment of the horse.

Coat is another key indication as to sound feeding or lack of it. A dull, dry coat that handles harshly means something, somewhere, along the line is wrong. The coat of a healthy, correctly fed horse should have a natural shine – a shine that comes from within, summer or winter, and a coat that handles softly, giving a supple feel as it moves freely over the flesh beneath. A stabled horse should be muscled up and firm if it is receiving hard food – that is corn; whereas one out at grass receiving no extra food will be soft – that is the flesh will feel podgy when pressed with the hand. The crest of the neck on a fit horse is hard and firm, one's fingers should not penetrate; whereas with an unfit, grass-fed horse the crest is normally soft, unless so gross that it is stiff with pure fat.

It is a fallacy to assert that a horse that has never been known to carry any flesh on its bones, is just habitually thin. Unless the horse has some incurable trouble that is beyond veterinary treatment – insidious pain is a great flesh remover – then correct, sound feeding should ensure restoration to good condition and maintaining it. I have proved this on my own rescue cases; and others, whose feeding I have advised on. Galavant, my 15.1hh Thoroughbred mare was a perfect example. For a year after her arrival it was hard to realise she was the same mare that had staggered out of the trailer on the evening of Friday, 7 August 1970 – the eve of her seventh birthday. Ragged, dirty, and with oozing cuts on her legs and hips, she had forgotten how to eat or drink in a stable, so we turned her out onto fresh, clean grass next to the house. By the Sunday we had cleaned her up and tidied her mane and tail – there was some hope she would live. A month later her skinny body was covered, and her scraggy neck resumed a respectable shape; her coat too, was beginning to shine, and her skin felt less taut – she was on the road to recovery. We had our problems – problems that always come with horses that are allowed to reach such a low ebb; but thanks to the never ending help of our veterinary surgeon, backed up by our blacksmith, Galavant became a fit, healthy mare again – a superb hunter who carried me for six seasons with the Duke of Beaufort's Hounds, before her past started to catch up on her. Retired to stud in 1976, she presented us with a very pretty brown filly on the night of Friday, 1 July 1977 – River Gipsy, by the HIS stallion River Poaching, but her condition was, despite all efforts, deteriorating; so, on Friday, 26 May 1978, in order to prevent her suffering further, she was with great sadness, put down – a few weeks short of her fifteenth birthday, to end for me nearly eight years of faithful companionship. River Gipsy though remains, and after a very shaky start, has really proved what sound feeding can achieve.

Cleanliness is the keynote to sound feeding. Without it one will get nowhere. Not only must all feeding stuffs be clean, free from mould and dust, but their place of storage must be kept in order too, by sweeping up daily, so that mouldy, musty food cannot contaminate the good stuff. Nor should vermin and other animals be allowed to soil food that horses are going to eat. Buckets, mangers, feed tins, hay nets, paddocks, stables – these must be kept absolutely clean, for dirt merely taints food and spreads disease.

When feeding, some basic rules must be observed if digestive upsets are to be avoided, and loss of condition prevented. Briefly they are as follows, and will be dealt with in detail later on.

(1) Water *before* feeding, never after
(2) Feed at regular times and intervals.
(3) Feed little and often, rather than one large feed.
(4) Feed plenty of bulk food to aid digestion.
(5) Do not work on a full stomach.
(6) Do not water or feed a hot tired horse until it has cooled off – then give water in small amounts and easily digested food, until recovered.
(7) Feed according to the work being done.
(8) Do not make sudden changes in diet.
(9) Weigh all food, never guess at amounts.
(10) Ensure all food is fresh, clean and of good quality.
(11) Wash out all buckets after mixing a feed; and mangers and feed tins daily.
(12) Give the correct amount of food for size and weight of horse.

5

Estimating a horse's weight is not easy for most owners. Remember though that height is not the sole governing factor in judging weight, body size is just as important. A 14 hh show pony with its light body will weigh far less than a pony of the same size of cob type; so too will a Thoroughbred, against a horse of the same size of hunter type. If in any doubt get your veterinary surgeon to give his estimate as to weight – after all it will be required for assessing the correct worm dose; or else put your horse over your local weighbridge.

Figure 1.1   BODY WEIGHT VERSUS DAILY FOOD REQUIREMENTS

Size (hands)	Average approximate body weight	Daily food intake
10·2 (000·0 cm)	250 lb (113·40 kg)	6¼ lb (2·83 kg)
11 (111·8 cm)	300 lb (136·08 kg)	7½ lb (3·40 kg)
11·2 (116·8 cm)	350 lb (158·76 kg)	8¾ lb (3·96 kg)
12 (121·9 cm)	400 lb (181·44 kg)	10 lb (4·53 kg)
12·2 (127 cm)	450 lb (204·12 kg)	11¼ lb (5·10 kg)
13 (132·1 cm)	500 lb (227 kg)	12½ lb (5·75 kg)
13.2 (137·2 cm)	600 lb (272 kg)	15 lb (6·81 kg)
14 (142·2 cm)	700 lb (318 kg)	17½ lb (8·00 kg)
14·2 (147·3 cm)	800 lb (363 kg)	20 lb (9·07 kg)
15 (TB) (152.4 cm)	950 lb (431 kg)	23¾ lb (10·87 kg)
15 (Hunter) (152·4 cm)	1,100 lb (499 kg)	27½ lb (12·50 kg)
15·2 (TB) (157·5 cm)	1,000 lb (454 kg)	25 lb (11·25 kg)
15·2 (Hunter) (157·5 cm)	1,250 lb (467 kg)	31¼ lb (14·10 kg)
16 (TB) (162·6 cm)	1,100 lb (499 kg)	27½ lb (12·50 kg)
16 (Hunter) and over) (162·6 cm)	1,400 lb (636 kg)	35 lb (15·88 kg)

The feeding chart (Figure 1.1) is a guide to food requirements, based on the fact that every horse requires 2½ per cent of its body weight in food per day to maintain condition. That is, 2½ lb (1·13 kg) of food for every 100 lb (45·36) of body weight, 25 lb (11·34 kg) of food if the horse weighs 1,000 lb (453·60 kg). Some people quote the figure of 3 per cent, or 3 lb (1·36 kg), of food for every 100 lb (45·36 kg) of body weight. This might be true for some horses in very hard work, who are burning up more food than a horse doing normal work. Some horses may refuse even the lower amount, so they have to be fed with great care, and extra nourishing food, to ensure that they receive the equivalent in food value of the larger diet.

Most rations refer to dry matter – that is minus moisture. Hay though dry in itself has a moisture content, and to get 17 lb (7·71 kg) of dry matter one has to feed 19½ lb (8·84 kg) of hay. Only when hay forms the whole of the diet does this factor have any real significance. The moisture content of corn is also small once it has dried out and is therefore of no consequence – and corn must be dry and hard before being fed to horses, otherwise it will cause digestive upsets by setting up fomentation in the horse's stomach, which in turn leads to colic (pain in the stomach – gut – which should always be treated as serious until proved otherwise). What does play an important part in making up a ration for an individual horse is the food value of each type of feeding stuff.

Ponies require the same standard and care in feeding as horses, but their origin must be remembered and their feed planned sensibly. Too rich food such as pasture or concentrates is harmful to them, so choose rations designed for ponies and remember to feed hay from December to April – and, in some cases, if very dry, from mid-summer until the autumn grass comes again. In bleak weather ponies will require an extra feed to the twice daily needed during the winter months.

Parasite control and teeth also play an important part in sound feeding and maintaining good condition. In the former category, lice which can suck a pint of blood from their host per day, and worms, in all their forms, must be kept under control or eliminated. Lice are worse some years than others, and a check must be kept for them in manes, tails and along the back, both of horses at grass, especially in the spring, and sometimes in the stable if an infected animal has been in before. If discovered, then it is wise to seek veterinary aid to eradicate them, and if necessary build up the strength of the horse again. Worms too, must be treated regularly under veterinary guidance, at intervals your veterinary surgeon will advise – in this way the best possible control will be obtained for your particular horse. An e.p.g. (egg per gramme count) should be taken at intervals to determine the worm burden the horse is carrying. Clean stables and paddocks are half the battle against worms and all parasites, which are merely expensive visitors, if allowed to remain.

Teeth, so often neglected, is another factor having a great deal of bearing on feeding and is the cause of much loss of condition. Should a horse be seen to drop food out of the side of its mouth while feeding ('quidding' as it is known) then the teeth must be examined by a veterinary surgeon with all speed. Teeth anyway require inspecting twice a year, in all age groups, and if found to be sharp or carry 'spurs' (as these sharp edges are sometimes known) they must be filed with a special rasp – which is also known as 'floating'.

The reason a horse's teeth must be filed or rasped lies in the fact the upper jaw is wider than the lower one, and the molars of the upper jaw have a downwards and outwards growth, while the lower molars have in contrast an inwards and upwards one, causing the outer edges of the upper molars (back teeth that grind the food) and the inner edges of the lower ones to become sharp, which in turn can then lacerate the insides of the cheeks and the sides of the tongue. Once this happens the horse will either refuse to eat, or else swallow part chewed food giving itself digestive upsets. (Teeth were one of the many factors for Galavant's appalling condition when she arrived.) Wolf teeth – small rudimentary teeth just in front of the first molars, are also a source of trouble, but should be removed by a veterinary surgeon with either a general or local anaesthetic according to which he deems necessary for the individual case. Sometimes they are so tight against the molars that, if not found young and allowed to become covered in tartar, they are extremely hard to discern.

One of my horses, Castania, developed wolf teeth and the condition showed itself when she reared at a combine harvester – she was 19-years-old then and always ridden in a double bridle. On examining her mouth on return, I found the loose tooth with an abscess behind it – once drained and healed, I rode her in future in a plain snaffle!

So much for the principles of feeding. The following chapters will, I hope, enable readers to understand the various feeding stuffs and enable them to work out a satisfactory diet sheet for their particular horse, thereby producing that true companionship which comes from feeding a horse well and maintaining its condition under all circumstances.

2 Water – the foremost essential

Water – H_2O, without which no horse can survive, is the one thing most grudged by many people. So often, a bucket or trough has either insufficient or even dirty water in it, but the person responsible will refuse to change or refill, until it is completely empty. In consequence the horse using that water is slowly dehydrating and starving for want of sufficient water. In ordinary weather the situation is serious enough, but in hot weather this sort of callousness is nothing short of extreme cruelty. Horses once treated in this manner will remain suspicious for a considerable time and every effort must be made to help them regain their confidence, so that they will drink freely again. In all probability they will also become very agitated every time their water bucket is removed from their box, even for refilling, or is allowed to become partly empty – this applies to field troughs as well, if not self-filling.

Water is the foremost essential and all horses regardless of how or where they are kept must have a plentiful supply of clean, fresh water at all times, or be given access to some at least three times a day in normal weather and far more frequently in hot. A horse will, under normal conditions, require 6 to 12 gallons (27·26 to 54·52l) a day – less when turned out on damp grass which has a high moisture content of its own, and more when the weather is hot, or they are being fed dry food, such as hay, corn etc. Mares in foal and with a foal at foot will also require more water than an ordinary horse. The bigger the horse,the more water it will require; nevertheless, regardless of size, at least 4 gallons (18·17l) should be available, in a clean receptacle, at any one time – small buckets are useless, and knock over far too easily.

When water is always available horses will seldom over-drink – it is quite common to see a horse go to its water supply in the middle of a feed, take a small drink, and return to finish its feed – this does no harm. It is wise though to refill all buckets before feeding, as horses will often take a fair-sized drink from a freshly filled bucket, even if their own bucket was already full. The maxim *always water before* feeding, never directly after (allow 1 to 2 hours after a feed before offering water again) is necessary as the horse's stomach is small and cannot cope with a full feed and several gallons of water simultaneously; the water would merely swell the food too fast and prevent digestion, causing colic.

It is harmful too, to allow a horse to drink freely while hot from exercise or work. A horse must first be cooled off – hence the reason why one should always walk a horse back to its stable after work, and not trot or canter back to the stable door. Offer the horse water that has had the chill removed (add boiling water to the cold water in the bucket), in very small quantities every 15 minutes until the horse is breathing normally and is no longer thirsty. Then, and only then, can a bucket be left with the horse in safety.

A horse's body contains about 50 per cent water when mature, and about 80 per cent when it is a newborn foal; without sufficient fluid horses' bodies cannot function properly. Deprive a horse of water and the blood, largely water, fails to carry the nutrients from the digestive system to the rest of the body, or collect up the waste products for their elimination through the skin (sweating) and kidneys (urine). It is rather like a river – keep the water level at the correct height and the river will flow freely, cleaning the river bed as it goes, so the whole area is clear; reduce that water, and very soon the debris within the water will be unable to pass freely and sink to the bottom, silting up the whole system until it becomes stagnant and a hotbed of disease and trouble.

Choice of water supply is also very important. Water can act as a carrier for poisons and contagious diseases. Pollution in some form or other is a very real risk these days if a natural water supply is used. Probably the only rivers and streams that are safe, are those high up on the mountains and moors, away from all industrial activities and modern farming; land these days is saturated with sprays and other chemicals to kill unwanted pests and diseases. If allowed to seep into a stream or river such chemicals can trigger off illness in some form or other, very often hard to identify as the cause is not immediately apparent. For this reason, in the majority of cases, unless you have a deep well, passed fit for human consumption, it is wise to use piped water.

Water varies from very soft to very hard. One end of the scale is deficient in Lime Salts, while very hard water can after a considerable time cause the formation of calculi in the intestine or bladder and upset digestion. Therefore medium water should be chosen for preference.

Paddocks require fairly large quantities of water laid on, otherwise horses will not have sufficient water for their needs. Troughs are the most usual, either with automatic filling, or filled by hand. With the former, care must be taken to see that the troughs are getting a steady supply of fresh water and that the ball-cock has not become defective. All troughs must be checked every day and cleaned out thoroughly once a week. To do this turn the water off, or tie up the ball-cock and then bail out the trough with a bucket – plastic is good – as it will slide along the bottom; scrub the sides and bottom and then remove the remains of the dirty water with a sponge, before refilling. If a hose is used, then do make sure it is the type that can be used for drinking water. (Some of the green garden hoses have a label with 'not to be used for potage', this means unsuitable for drinking water!)

All troughs must have round corners and should be made of concrete or metal. Some of the modern troughs are very dangerous and must have the top edges boxed in, or the corners protected somehow. This will prevent the horse banging and cuttings its legs on the corners. Troughs hold from 30 gallons (136·30l) upwards. If a large trough is not available, then an 8 gallon (36·34l) flat bottomed feeding bowl is the next best thing. This will not be knocked over so easily and requires only filling twice a day for one horse. The special heavy-duty plastic bowls designed to fit into a tyre are even more stable. Some advocate the use of household dustbins – I personally do not like them, and consider them potentially dangerous. They are too deep and narrow for my liking; the horse has a long way to push its head down. The 18 gallon (81·78l) plastic water trough is far safer.

Water for *stabled* horses is now normally provided by either automatic bowls or by buckets kept permanently in the stable. Automatic bowls come in either metal or plastic, fitted with a filling device that is operated by the horse pushing its nose against a flange in order to obtain water, or by a concealed valve that shuts off when the horse is not drinking and switches on when it is – the latter is the better type as many horses have sensitive noses and will not press hard enough to obtain water. Not every horse will use these bowls, and care must be taken with their siting for they can cause an obstruction for the horse to knock into or get caught up against. Admittedly they mean a horse should, if the bowl is not choked up, have a free supply of fresh water and cannot drink too much, too fast; against this one has no way in which to tell how much water a horse is drinking or not drinking as the case may be – a key factor to a horse's well being or lack of it. With the flange type, a horse runs the risk of catching its tongue or lip, which could be very serious.

Personally, I prefer my horses not to use automatic bowls. Buckets, though requiring more work as one has to fill them several times a day, are better. I always use stable buckets of the wide-bottomed type. They hold 4 gallons (18.17l) and are far more stable than the ordinary bucket, giving plenty of room for the horse's muzzle. Like all plastic buckets, however, their handles are light and do not lie so safely round the rim, and the horse can pick the empty bucket up in its teeth by the hollow rim, which the old type metal buckets do not possess. These metal buckets are much heavier (though lighter than the old fashioned wooden bucket) and will not shift on the floor when partly empty, therefore being much safer, especially for foals. The modern plastic bucket is not so safe, for not only could a foal get its small head through the handle, but its tiny, narrow jaw could get wedged under the hollow rim. A problem that could still occur with the excellent new heavy-duty, wide-bottomed, 5¼ gallon (23·85l) buckets, which have eliminated many of the problems of the older type plastic bucket.

I have found the safest answer lies in using a feeding bowl which is wide-bottomed and has no hollow rim or handle, and cannot be knocked over. It also holds enough for two horses' requirements, being of 8 gallons (36.34 l) capacity. I bury my bowls and buckets in straw for good reasons – to protect young legs, and in freezing conditions to prevent the water icing up. Frost is a hazard that must be contended with regarding drinking water. Outside troughs must have their ice broken at frequent intervals and, if necessary, a separate supply provided; inside, an eye must be kept on all pipes feeding automatic bowls, for these can easily freeze leaving the horse without water. Should they freeze, then buckets must be provided, preferably with chilled water.

Bucket holders are becoming popular with many owners, as they prevent the ordinary, narrow-bottomed plastic bucket being knocked over; but should the horse lift the bucket out, or the owner leave it out, then the holder merely forms a serious risk hazard – horses have a habit of putting their legs in all the wrong places and could easily break one if caught up through the holder. All stables should be free of projections and these holders form such a projection; for these reasons I would not use them myself.

Filling buckets can be done in several ways. By dipping into a central trough – not to be recommended as it can spread disease; by using a hose, now becoming fashionable, but it must mean everywhere around gets very wet in the process; and thirdly, directly from a tap. This last method means carrying the bucket to and from the stable, but the bucket does get rinsed out with running water, and therefore is by far the cleanest way. By all means top up with another bucket if necessary, but remember only use a bucket that no other horse has drunk from or else you could be passing on trouble that is in the incubation stage.

If one can, then it is labour saving to have more than one tap, and to have them placed outside the boxes to save walking miles with full buckets. Bowls have to be bailed out, then removed for rinsing at least once a day and refilled. They hold two buckets of water, and can be topped up in between their complete changes morning and evening. Whatever type of receptacle used, it must be scrubbed out once a day.

Horses living in either an open yard with shed attached or in an enclosed yard will require water laid on or provided in a hand-filled trough. These troughs can be smaller than those used in a field, but must be of sufficient size for the number of horses using them, and sited in such a way as to prevent the horses getting cornered alongside them.

Foals will drink from an early age if given the chance, so see that a supply is available low down within their reach. Make sure there is no chance of their being caught up in any way when trying to drink or play with the water – a game they will indulge in for hours!

Should your horse be tethered, then water must be placed on the outer perimeter. An 8 gallon (36·34 l) feeding bowl would be suitable, at such a distance that the horse can reach the water with ease, but not get its tether caught on it.

When travelling horses, one must take along a supply of fresh, clean water for them to drink. A plastic, 5 gallon (22·71 l) water carrier, though heavy when full, is the most suitable. Only use carriers bought for the purpose, for those used previously for some other liquid could taint the water. To use a common trough at a show is asking for infection, and it is only safe to use water from a running tap connected direct to mains supply. Some horses will refuse strange water – they can 'taste' water more than most animals, so it is always wise to have a supply with one. The heavy-duty plastic bucket, with one flat side to enable it to be hung against a wall, is very useful in a horse-box while waiting after classes as it allows the horse to drink at leisure.

3 Roughage

The horse is a herbivorous creature, which in the wild lives on rough herbage, grazing over wide tracts of ground to obtain its food. Hill ponies select by instinct the type of grazing they require to fulfil their nutritional requirements, which enables them under normal weather conditions to remain fit and healthy – they eat, and exercise.

On the other hand our own horses are kept in enclosed areas of varying size and quality, and therefore have no choice as to what they will eat, as the ponies in the wild do. Nor do our horses have to exercise themselves in order to obtain their food, unless kept on sparse pasture. In summer, throughout May, June and July, there is normally an abundance of fresh, lush grass, so the horse merely eats, sleeps, and eats again, getting grossly over-fat unless grazing is restricted.

Digestion

Young grass is tender and easily digested, but old grass becomes fibrous and this is far harder for a horse to digest. Before going further we must understand a little about the horse's digestive system.

Horses, like cows, can live on grass and hay (dried grass), but the horse does not chew the cud, nor does it have a compound stomach (more than one) for the breakdown of fibrous plant material to produce nutrients. The horse's stomach is simple, like that of a human or a dog, but while we cannot digest hay, the horse can by virtue of its special type of large intestine – in fact the horse has a unique digestive system.

The horse's food has a long and tortuous journey. First the

strong upper lip and lower lip grasp the grass and pass it back between the front teeth – incisor teeth, six in each jaw, which nip off the grass close to the ground – closer than a cow; this grass is then passed back via the tongue (corn is taken by the lips direct to the tongue; and hay grasped by the teeth and passed back), to the grinding teeth at the back – molars, broad, flat, rough surfaced teeth that number six a side, top and bottom, making 24 in all. Here the food is ground and chewed to a mass and mixed with saliva from the salivary glands in the mouth.

Failure to chew thoroughly, whether from neglected teeth, laziness, greediness (bolting) or whatever, leads to the swallowing of partly prepared food which is hard for the horse to digest and could either lead to colic or pass along without the nutrients being fully extracted on the way. From the mouth, the chewed food then passes through the pharynx – a chamber at the back of the mouth common to both the windpipe and the oesophagus – gullet, which is a one-way system; rendering it virtually impossible for a horse to vomit, and should it try the results could be drastic. Because of this dual chamber great care must be taken to ensure foods and liquids never enter the windpipe – if they did the horse would die. Once in the gullet, the food is conveyed to the stomach – one can see the balls of food passing down the left side of the neck, and once there the process of digestion starts. The horse's stomach is very small and lies directly against the diaphragm which guards the lungs. Too much food at this stage and digestion will be hurried, or the stomach over-loaded, which means, should the horse be asked to work, that pressure from the distended, full stomach will be exerted upon the diaphragm and impede the full expansion of the lungs.

While in the stomach the food is mingled with stomach juices, and reduced to a pulp – the juices now containing a large part of the nutrients of the food are passed into the small intestine to undergo further mixing and movement. Once this part of the process has been completed a good deal of absorption takes place, through the gut wall, of nutrients to nourish the horse's body. At intervals the fibrous parts of the horse's food are passed straight through to the caecum of the large intestine – a sac like part of the alimentary tract which holds the food and kneads and churns it around, prior to sending it upon its journey through the large and small colons finally to reach the rectum. The more fibrous parts of the food can remain in the caecum for 24 hours or even 36 hours. It is at this point of digestion that, if something goes wrong, the food can pack (impaction) and obstructive colic occurs. The food, be it fibrous like hay and the husk (outside coating) of oats; or succulent like grass, roots and apples, should by now have reached a thoroughly soft state thanks to the action of enzymes (complex organic chemical compounds) that break up nutrients (food-stuff) into simple compounds that can be absorbed into the system. This is how the horse gets its nourishment be it protein, starches, sugars, fats, vitamins or minerals; or any of the other substances horses require and can obtain from their food. That part of the food which cannot be broken up and absorbed is passed along, into the rectum and evacuated – the horse passing droppings or faeces about twelve times a day.

As can be seen it is a long process that if disturbed will throw the whole 'mechanism' out of timing, and if over-loaded will merely work at below its real potential (that is, the horse will not be obtaining full benefit from the food received) or else grind to a halt like the engine of a car that has been asked too much of. Over-load it and it stalls – so too a horse's stomach will stall and this is when digestive trouble starts to brew and if left unattended, will boil causing colic.

Should a horse swallow objects that can get lodged in its gullet, then it will choke and unlike a human or a dog it cannot bring it back.

This is only a brief description of the digestion of the horse and I have not gone into detail, as I believe to do so will only serve to confuse the ordinary owner. A word though will not be out of place concerning the fluids of the body. The blood having picked up the required nutrients from absorption through the gut wall, then passes through the kidneys at one stage of its journey round the body. Here waste products and water are extracted from the blood stream and excreted as urine. Analysis of urine will indicate any poisons or defects present in the horse's system should there be any question as to its well being, and which is not apparent by normal study of the horse.

Grass

So much for how the horse eats. Grass is the basic food horses live on and require, either in its natural state or made into hay, in order to have sufficient bulk or roughage to ensure proper digestion. Though a horse can live on roughage alone, providing it has water, it cannot live on concentrates (corn, etc.), without a certain percentage of roughage to ensure correct digestion.

The better the quality of grass, the more nourishment there is in it. The length of grass is no indication as to its quality. Long grass may look plentiful, but be of little or no use to the horse – once grass has flowered the feed value starts to diminish. Coarse, rank grass is not only bitter to taste, but also indigestible – ponies being better able to digest such grass than Thoroughbreds. Therefore, regardless of the time of year, horses' pasture should be kept topped (cut with a 'Hayter'-type cutter or one that does not chew up the grass and leave it in balls which can be highly dangerous if eaten) to a height of about 2 to 4 inches (5 to 10.16 cm). This topping ensures fresh growth so that the whole paddock will be grazed evenly; it also prevents the weeds seeding and helps cut them down. It is essential to maintain a good 'bottom' to the grass, that is thickness at the roots, so that when the horse walks over the grass it is not damaging the tender roots near the surface. In summer during May, June and July, and sometimes as early as April, the grass will be growing so fast it will be necessary to top the paddocks once a week. In this way I have kept even a half acre paddock serviceable for the whole summer.

Though one can keep horses on a small acreage, it is not to be recommended. Admittedly I only had just a half acre (0.20 ha) paddock for the last 25 years since leaving our farm; but to keep a horse correctly one should have 2 acres (0.80 ha) per horse, this allows for resting one half while the other half is grazed. Horses living out summer and winter require a greater acreage than those just out during the summer months, when the grass is growing and has its maximum nutritional value. Ponies can live on grass, even poor grass, far better than horses, who, if well bred, require a far higher standard of nutrition than ponies or horses of cob type, who have a habit of getting too fat, on remarkably little grass. These customers must have their grazing restricted during the months when the grass is growing, being shut up in a stable, yard or shed – they must have shade from the sun and water to drink, for part of each day, being allowed to graze for two hours at a time, and then being shut up for a spell and given another two hours. How long they are out depends on how fat they are getting. Too much rich grass leads to laminitis – also known as founders or fever in the feet. This is an allergy that can be triggered off by too much protein – clover is a culprit, and so too, are other factors, but its relation to grass is what we are concerned with here. The answer lies with the owner who should never let a horse at grass get gross, especially ponies and cobs.

In winter, or very dry weather, it is often necessary to feed more food than the grazing can provide – burnt up grass has no nourishment. But dried up grass in winter will provide some roughage for ponies if additional food is provided as well. Water lying on paddocks is another factor to be contended with. The winter of 1977/8 was one of the worst I can remember, and our paddock finally said 'enough'. Grazed by day, by both Galavant and the growing River Gipsy, it was standing water by the end of October and from November onwards the roots of the grass were permanently under water, so that by the New Year it was an ever deepening sea of mud. This type of grazing is useless for horses and ours only went out for two hours a day in order to exercise, receiving hay to keep them content at the same time. I had nowhere else to put them, if I had I would never have used it.

The choice of grasses in a paddock is most important. They must be nourishing, sweet tasting and at the same time able to withstand a horse walking and moving around. The best is perennial rye grass, which also makes some of the best hay. Timothy is another excellent grass, but not very good at fighting back against other grasses, which after a year or so tend to make it die out of the pasture. It is a grass too, if allowed to grow for too long, that tends to become very 'stalky' or fibrous, in which state it is not so easily digested. Nevertheless, timothy, provided it is grazed or cut young for hay, is an excellent grass. Smooth-stalked grasses and meadow fescues; plus cocksfoot and foxtails all help to give a good grazing mixture and offer variety. The inclusion of clover, wild white is a favourite, is normally done to provide nitrogen, and in small quantities is an asset, but it has a nasty habit of taking over and killing off the other grasses that are so valuable. Vetches are also welcome, and the native ponies in the wild have a wide choice and can find these nice extras for themselves. One word of warning regarding pastures: weeds will grow – most are harmless, but some like ragwort are deadly and must be pulled out by the roots, removed (every tiny leaf, dead or alive) and burnt. Ragwort will grow to a variety of heights. All droppings should be removed from paddocks daily – twice a day with small fields, to reduce the risk of worm infestation and sour pasture.

Fresh Grass

Fresh grass can be fed in many ways. The normal way is by grazing, when the horse has complete freedom to move at will over the whole area. If the horse is stabled then it can be led out on a lead rein, attached either to a headcollar if quiet, or safer, a lungeing cavesson, for a spell each day to pick grass from the sides of quiet roads or lanes, or some suitable patch of clean grass. Alternatively, a horse can be tethered – attached by a long chain (never rope) to a metal stake in the ground, round which it will revolve by means of swivels in the chain. A strong leather headcollar or neck collar is necessary, and horses must be inspected frequently and their patch moved, to ensure fresh grass and shade, plus water within reach. Green feed, long cut grass, is useful for stabled horses in summer or when grass is short. Lucerne is useful as green feed. Never though feed lawn mowings – these ball up in the horse's stomach; and also heat very fast. Grass once it has started to heat is unsafe for horses and produces colic. All grass must be fed fresh cut within an hour, to avoid fermentation setting in, once it has it is unsafe and must be thrown away.

Hay

Hay is dried young grass, cut before the grasses have come into full flower, left on the ground to first wilt and then dry in the fresh air and sunshine, being turned and tossed by machine (by hand in the old days) until quite dry and crisp to handle. It is the staple diet of all horses throughout the winter months and during the rest of the year when there is either insufficient grass to maintain them, or the horse is stabled. Hay once made can be either ricked – old fashioned but still the best as the hay can then mature thoroughly, or baled – large, small, round, bales come in all shapes and sizes. Ricked hay has to be cut out of the rick and either trussed (cut into parcels and tied by hand) or baled from the rick. Unless one makes one's own hay, one seldom finds it these days – 1955 was the last year I was able to buy it. Baled hay can be satisfactory, but it has a habit of forming mouldy patches in its middle – hay that is mouldy *must never* be fed as it can cause serious digestive upsets. Dusty hay, or hay that has been wet is also not good for horses. Mow-burnt hay – hay that has over-heated almost to the point of firing – can easily heat to such an extent that the whole rick (baled or loose) can go up in flames. It is very dark brown in colour, has a toasted smell about it and has little feeding value left. Nowadays hay is also 'barn' dried, that is the bales are made up sooner than normal and taken into a barn, stacked in such a way as to allow air to pass between them and then dried out by hot air. This hay is expensive but contains a higher feeding value than most outside dried hay, and it is not so dependent on the weather. Rain on hay merely spoils it, washing much of the goodness out of it. Hay that has been rained on after cutting, especially after it has been turned, will in all probability go mouldy or dusty in the bale, with a musty smell – this hay is useless, in fact harmful. Bad hay also leads to respiratory trouble, so great care must be taken only to feed the highest quality hay that has been well saved – that is made without rain.

A word of serious warning: in recent years hay preservatives have become the vogue with many farmers. These preservatives – there are several different makes on the market – contain chemicals which retard or prevent the formation of mould on hay and are applied to the sward (cut grass) before baling. As yet very little is known regarding the effects this will have on horses. Propionic acid is one chemical used and this is known to destroy vitamin E and reduce the value of all other vitamins. Now this in itself could be serious if additional vitamins were not fed and could be costly if vitamin E supplement had to be given – this vitamin being essential for muscle formation and fertility. As any feeding of deficient products takes time, even years, to show the final end results, and this preservative has been produced largely with the feeding of farm livestock and not horses in mind, it is only wise to think very carefully before using treated hay. After all, our horses have a very different digestive system to a cow and we expect our horses to exert themselves in such a way as to put their muscles to the maximum stress at times. There are enough unsound horses already without our adding to their numbers. Untreated hay can be found and is a far safer buy until more research on the feeding of treated hay has been carried out in relation to effects, for good or bad, on horses.

Hay can be taken (cut) from either permanent pasture – grass fields that are never ploughed up, but left as grass from one year to the next or from specially sown fields designed to produce a crop of hay of selected grass, or grasses. The former is known as meadow hay, while the later is termed seed or mixture hay.

MEADOW HAY can vary in quality considerably according to the type of land it is grown on; and ranges from very soft to that which in a good year can be graded with seed hay for quality and texture. Some parts of the country will term meadow hay by other names (over in the Cotswolds it is known as *English hay*) so if in doubt ask what type of pasture it is from. Of the meadow hays, *Upland* is best as this is taken from dry land and should contain a good mixture of quality grasses together with herbage – this in its turn can be vetches, or weeds, which are less desirable. *Lowland hay* is taken from low-lying land that is often very wet in winter and the quality of the grasses tend to be poor, and the herbage more of the weed variety or wild flowers. Lastly we have that hay taken from *Water Meadows*, and here the hay is seldom of a quality suitable for horses.

SEED or MIXTURE HAY is preferable as it is free from weeds and much cleaner – the quality too is normally higher if taken young with the sap running. Rye grass is one of the most popular, and is liked by horses as it is crisp and easy to chew. To form mixture hay, red clover is often included. If cut young, before becoming stalky – coarse and fibrous – and well dried through, it is excellent, the only snag being it often heats and then turns mouldy or musty, ruining the whole crop or that part that is affected, for mouldy patches can be found within what looks like a sound bale. Mouldy or musty hay must *never* be fed to horses, not only will it affect their digestion, but also their wind. Timothy grass is another either used on its own to produce seed hay or included in a mixture – an excellent grass, but tends to turn coarse and fibrous if not cut young. *Clover*, red clover; *Sainfoin*, a member of the trefoil family; and *Alfalfa* – Lucerne, are all valuable as hay owing to their very high protein value; being rich they require only feeding in limited quantities, thereby making them eminently suitable for racehorses, eventers in hard work and breeding stock whose bulk has to be restricted.

Fine hay is unsuitable for horses as it balls in their mouth, so choose a sample with a crispness and that sweet aroma that denotes good hay. Cut young, the grass will retain its colour and leaf, enabling the hay to retain its fullest feeding value.

MEADOW HAY ranges in colour from fresh green through to a paler, browny green; whereas SEED HAY is a yellowish green, through to a warm shade of light brown. Dark brown denotes 'mowburnt' and means over-heating with a smell of toasted hay.

The protein value of hay varies from as low as 5 per cent to as high as 15 per cent in a top-class sample. The moisture content also varies – in growing grass the moisture content is approximately 80 per cent, but for hay this must be reduced to below 20 per cent. Good hay should have a moisture content on leaving the field of around 15 per cent if it is not going to over-heat – nevertheless, all hay will dry out once ricked or baled, therefore giving a weight loss to hay 'bought off the field', that is while it is still growing or freshly baled, so that the ton (tonne) of hay purchased will, once dried right out, probably weigh quite a bit less; so allowances must be made when purchasing off the field, or else you will run out of hay before the following year.

Never feed new hay, but wait at least until it has cooled right off and attained its crispness. Strictly speaking hay should be six months old before being fed, but with the hay shortage of recent years, this is not always possible, and fresh hay has had to be used. If you must use fresh hay – then open the bale, spread it out on the floor of an airy shed; shaking up enough for the next 24 hours. Leave for 24 hours and then if crisp this can

23

be used, but it must feel like old hay first; and introduce in small quantities, otherwise trouble will ensue. I have used hay so treated on more than one occasion with no trouble, but watch the horses for scouring or signs of discomfort, and if in doubt stop feeding it.

STORING HAY is important too. A large airy Dutch barn, closed on three sides, is best for large quantities, but the small owner can house the hay and straw satisfactorily in an open shed providing a black plastic rick sheet is spread over the floor first to prevent rising moisture. Keep the shed tidy and watch out in winter for snow blowing in – if it does, cover the hay. A feed house near the stables for hay and straw in use is an asset, as one can also fill and store the hay nets for the day, by hanging them on the wall. Sweep up and tidy the shed daily – dirt and dust merely lead to trouble. Mice and other vermin require a stable cat, or trap (break-back type) to control them – never let cat and trap come in contact, or the cat will be injured. Rat poison is *never* allowed near our buildings, for if a rat or mouse took the bait and then 'soiled' on the hay or feeding stuffs, the food would become contaminated. *Warfarin* is a deadly poison which passes out from the body with the urine, and would merely soak into the food, to be consumed in turn by the horses, which if taken in any quantity could prove fatal or cause serious illness.

No, play safe and use a good cat or trap.

Dust-free 'hay', *HorseHage*, is a product designed for horses with allergy problems. It is dust and mould-spore free when used in accordance with the manufacturer's instructions. It is made from the same types of grasses as hay, but the grass is cut young and dried to the halfway stage and then baled. The bales are then treated by compression to less than half their normal size so that no heating can take place, and packed into strong plastic bags that are airtight. Once opened, the bag must be used within a few days. *Never* use a bag that has been damaged in anyway. *Never* store on straw or old hay, but on a smooth surface like a plastic sheet. Feed according to instructions.

This also applies to *ProPack* another product on the same lines and *Hygrass* – which differs in that it starts life as made hay and then is 'cooked' and impregnated with a protein additive. *HorseHage* and *ProPack* are additive free.

Dried Grass

Dried grass, is taken straight off the field and artificially dried, thereby retaining its food value and colour. A useful feed for horses, but should be used with care, especially for ponies as too much could lead to laminitis.

Silage

Silage is grass removed from the field and then made into a clamp, where it then matures. Really a cattle feed, but used now for horses by some people, but ensure no harmful additive has been used. If in doubt do not feed.

Straw

Straw is the stalk of cereal plants, once the grain has been thrashed out of it. *Wheat* is too fibrous for feeding. Spring wheat is softer than winter wheat. *Barley* is used for cattle and is fed to horses, but beware of the awns (spiky whiskers). *Oat*, if of clean quality, can be fed either long or chopped. Preferable to poor hay.

4 Energy foods

Energy foods are those designated to produce muscle power and energy in the horse, while at the same time creating body warmth, without which no horse will work well.

Natural foodstuffs are made up of carbohydrates, proteins, fats, fibre and water, together with minerals and some vitamins. While grass will provide all these things, a horse has to eat a vast quantity to gain the required nutrients for its daily needs; with energy foods, as I have termed them, they can derive the required amounts from eating a considerably smaller quantity – in short they are *concentrates*, hence the reason they are collectively known as such.

Carbohydrates

The major source of energy, carbohydrates include starches, sugars and cellulose (fibre). Oats, barley and maize contain about 60 per cent sugar and starch, which is why they come under the heading of concentrates. The cellulose comes from the fibrous part of the hulls (outer jacket) of oats and barley, and is also present in bran, which is the skin of wheat under the outer hull, before the kernel which is ground into flour.

Protein

The all-important factor in feeding horses, protein is essential for producing healthy muscle; its prime object being to form and repair tissue. It also plays its role in the formation of sound, healthy bone, blood, skin, hair and hooves. Withhold adequate protein from the horse's diet and the horse will suffer from weak muscles and a heart that is unable to withstand the rigours of proper training and work. Hearts are after all merely lumps of muscle that act as pumps for the blood supply of the whole body and a poor muscle will lead to inadequate pumping and circulation.

Fats

Fats are necessary for the absorption of certain fat soluble vitamins. In its natural state fat is not easily digested by the horse, so to overcome this some means of providing a digestible oil must be found – linseed and milk pellets are useful in this respect. Oils (fats) are present in small quantities in many natural foods and compounded ones.

Amino-acids

According to *Black's Veterinary Dictionary* there are 24 principal ones and constitute all the proteins in the animal and vegetable world.

The name amino-acid is that which is given to the substances derived from the ultimate products of digestion of protein foods, and from which the protein materials of the body are again built up. As with a child's set of building bricks, these amino-acids can be built up into many different 'buildings' (proteins in this case) and then broken down again into bricks (or back into amino-acids in our case) only to be used again and rebuilt in a different design or, with us, as a new protein or proteins.

With animals any surplus amino-acids are rendered harmless in the body and passed out in the urine or faeces. Glycine, alanine, and cystine, together with other amino-acids can be oxidised into glucose and are called glucogenic. Leucine, isoleucine, phenyl-alanine and tyrosine are known as ketogenic. Tryptophane, lysine, arginine, histidine, theonine, valine and methionine all go to form the 'essential' amino-acids, known as such for without their presence in the diet life cannot be sustained. Lysine has its importance in the fact that it is necessary for both growth and production of milk in all animals. tryptophane is an equal necessity for growth of all cells and normal development. Arginine and histidine have their role in connection with the bloodstream, keeping it normal and healthy, besides having other complex functions.

Other amino-acids all have their own functions. When feeding horses we tend to use foods that are deficient in lysine and methionine – grain ration of stabled horses being responsible for this, for oats, flaked maize and barley, mixed with bran, and in many cases backed up by sugar-beet pulp, do not exactly provide on their own the required levels of amino-acids, for though the deficiency of tryptophane, threonine and histidine is not so overall as the first two mentioned, it is present to a greater or lesser degree, and the level of leucine can be termed satisfactory, though to rectify matters a 'grain' balancer is required.

Though horses can and do live on grass alone (or when grass in its growing state is not available, hay) no horse can be made really fit and capable of the work we ask of them if grass is their only food. They require energy foods, namely corn or concentrates in some form or other. When choosing cereals go for good, clean samples, that smell sweet and rattle in one's hand.

The plumper the grain the more nourishing centre it has – and this is where the food value lies. This kernel, the soft creamy centre of the growing cereal grain that hardens and dries out once ripe and ready for harvesting, is largly composed of carbohydrates in the form of starch. It is this starch which supplies the horse with the required energy, and gives cereals their feeding value for horses. Their protein content is not high, averaging about 8.5 per cent for oats, maize and barley. But with a high starch content, cereals form the basis for horse rations, the protein being supplied by the addition of feeding stuffs known to be high in that respect, inclusion of which helps to balance out the diet to the right protein content. The higher the percentage of protein in a diet, the higher the feeding and nutritional value of that ration.

Oats

The principal cereal fed to horses in Britain, oats are also fed in many parts of the world. Grown best in moist climates with drier weather at ripening time, the best oats are said to come from Scotland, though in truth the year I went to the expense of feeding Scotch oats, I was getting no better a sample than oats I could buy off a local farm within our Hunt. The Scotch oats had been damped to crush, and went mouldy and green before I had had them a week, while the local oats were plump, clean and sweet smelling and I knew them to be free of all preservatives – for like hay, corn is now treated with propionic acid to prevent it going mouldy. The moisture content of corn should be less than 16 per cent, above this it normally gets treated, some lower samples may be treated too, so ensure you buy untreated oats if you can.

Oats can also come from Canada (some trainers I believe use imported oats) and from Australia, but these are expensive compared with home-grown cereals. The colour of oats can vary too, white oats are usually chosen and the sample should be shiny, but black oats in fact are only from another breed of oat. Some years the grain will get weather stained; providing the stain is only on the outer husk, and has not gone right through the oat, then the oat should be acceptable. Most corn is now harvested by combine and taken direct to a corn drier where it is dried by having its moisture content extracted till it reaches a level at which it will keep. As heat is used to dry, the corn tends to lose some of its vitamin value as compared with the old method of cutting and stooking in the field for three Sundays and then ricking till Christmas before thrashing it out. Quicker now, but probably no better.

Oats can be fed in one of four ways.

(1) Whole. Here the grain is used as it comes or having been 'clipped', that is, had its whiskery tail removed and also part of its outer husk (hull), the object of this being to remove part of the fibre content as this fibre is not of great feed value.

(2) Cracked or bruised. The advantage of bruising oats lies in the fact that the kernel is rather hard to crack open and some horses, if they fail to chew enough merely swallow the oats whole and then fail to extract the nutrients from them. If split open the internal juices can get to work.

(3) Crushed. Crimped or rolled, this is bruising taken a stage further, and the oats come out flattened having passed through much tighter metal rollers. Rolled oats are in fact

taken a stage further still and look rather like porridge oats which are much bulkier, but easier to digest and for some horses the answer.

Which oat one chooses depends largely on the horse and the work it is doing and the quantity of oats it should eat. The greater the quantity, the less the bulk required. No two samples of oats will weigh the same so every new sackful must be weighed, if weighing is not carried out at every feed.

(4) Cooked. These are soaked overnight and brought to the boil next morning, then simmered till the whole oats will form a jelly. Excellent for sick horses and those that need tempting or have a shy appetite, as cooked oats are easily digested. They also will help put flesh on a poor horse.

Barley

Even higher in starch than oats, barley is very fattening and, cooked to jelly in the same way as oats, is useful for putting on flesh on either thin horses, or building show and sale stock. (For some unknown reason people now turn out this stock looking like prime beef cattle – which after all is the principal use of barley for cattle and pigs to make them ready for market.) Too much barley in a horse's ration can cause colic and affect the kidneys.

Barley can be used whole. A hard grain, whole barley can only be fed boiled, which makes it easily digested and, when used in small quantities, is harmless, in fact of benefit to many horses. Crushed or rolled barley has been either put through a crusher while still holding a high moisture content (in which case the sample has quite likely been treated with proprionic acid in order to ensure it will keep) or else rolled by steam rollers (steam is ejected over the grain as it passes through to soften the grain and make it possible to roll out thinly). Once rolled it is then dried off again ready for sale and use.

In its crushed or rolled state barley can be fed as part of the corn ration, but only in small quantities. There is a marked tendency to over-feed barley or replace oats with barley in the mistaken idea that horses do not play up so much on barley; ¾lb (340g) of barley = 1lb (454g) of oats. Barley is a main constituent of horse nuts, so if nuts are included in a ration then the horse is probably receiving all the barley it requires, after all we are not producing prize porkers or beef cattle but horses capable of exerting themselves in many cases to the full over an extended period of time.

Maize

Indian corn or just corn, maize is a sweet, highly concentrate supply of starch that in its flaked state is highly acceptable to horses who love it. Owing to its high concentration of starch it must not be over-fed, ½lb (0–22 kg) a day is sufficient for a small horse.

In order to make the flakes, the whole maize (just the yellow kernel) is cooked and passed through rollers to flatten it into flakes that are then dried again to the crispness that we know. Like our breakfast cornflakes, they are highly palatable and excellent for putting flesh on poor horses and maintaining body heat in winter. I am a great believer in feeding flaked maize in winter, but in summer one must be careful as the horse's system could become over-heated.

Compounded feed-nuts and coarse mix

With dope testing requiring an owner to ensure that they do not feed any forbidden substance, even accidentally, the top firms are manufacturing compounded feeds in special factories for racehorses and eventers. Therefore any owner whose horses are likely to have to undergo a routine dope test after racing, jumping, eventing or showing, should only feed nuts and coarse mix labelled as suitable for a particular activity.

Compounded feeds are mixed with either molasses or (what one top firm now uses) Maltrose Syrup, which is a pure wheat syrup containing 75 per cent sugars. Many of the feeds now contain micronised cereals – that is, the grain is cooked by the same means as a domestic microwave and then rolled, rendering former grains, that were too hard and unsuitable, digestible. Wheat, peas, barley, soya and maize all come into this category and will be found in the various mixes along with locust bean, linseed and so on. Micronising removes the trypsin inhibitor in soya beans.

Nuts

A compounded feed made up into nuts, cubes or pencils of varying sizes. To make these all the various foodstuffs are ground to a fine meal and then compressed into the shapes that we know.

These nuts also carry a full range of vitamins and minerals, so supplying all the horse requires. Manufactured in different grades to suit horses with different work programmes, they offer the owner a feed that is always matched for quality, easy to dish out, but one which he cannot vary or mix easily with any other type of feed, unless used as only part of a diet. They have their advantages but also an equal number of disadvantages, one of which is that should a horse bolt these nuts without chewing, then a mushy mass collects in its stomach. This mass is very hard for the horse to digest; should the horse have a full feed of nuts and then be turned out onto wet pasture or allowed to drink from a field tank (they will often take a long drink from a field supply, having refused their own in the stable), the nuts, which are very dry in composition, will swell excessively into an undigestible mass, causing colic or a blockage. Some have even died. Horses on a diet of nuts alone will require far more water to drink than horses on a normal diet that contains moisture.

To assess the value of nuts look at the label on the bag which will give percentages for oil, protein and fibre – the higher the fibre content the lower the protein. Though the names of the various nuts manufactured vary – High Protein, Racehorse, and so on, all refer to the nuts carrying 14 per cent approximately of protein and below 10 per cent of fibre. The high fibre, 17 per cent, and low protein, 10 per cent, are intended for horses doing ordinary hacking and similar work, also children's ponies, and are normally known as Horse and Pony Nuts. For breeding stock the Stud Nut has been formulated and carries 15 per cent protein, 6 per cent fibre and like the Racehorse type of nut, 3½ per cent oil. The Horse and Pony type carries only 2½ per cent oil; which is the same as the Complete Nut.

Now the first three types of nuts are compounded so as to let the owner feed hay in addition to the nuts, but with the Complete Nut the owner is supposed to feed these and these alone – carrying 10 per cent protein and 20 per cent fibre, but if required one of the protein supplementary nuts can be added to raise the protein value of the feed – but the object is to eliminate all other feeding stuffs. The only class of horse I can see benefiting from such a diet would be those with some allergy which prevents them from receiving conventional food. Many people I know use them for horses at grass, but then they are being mixed with natural roughage.

Feeding Blocks

Similar in manufacture to nuts (for grain and other feeding stuffs are ground up and mixed into the correct proportions before being compressed into blocks) feeding blocks are placed in a suitable container in the field and the horse licks off the amount it requires per day. For out wintering stock they are a great help and I have seen horses look very well fed this way with hay ad lib for roughage. Breeding stock and Thorough-breds might require an additional feed of conventional type, but the analysis of oil 2·2 per cent, protein 13·5 per cent and fibre 4 per cent is such that ordinary horses should be adequately fed in this way. Their advantage over nuts lies in the fact that the horse licks the nourishment off the block and swallows it mixed with saliva in the form of a liquid, which then mixes with the hay or grass eaten before and after the licking session. In this way it is far less likely to cause a blockage than nuts. The old type feeding blocks carried a protein of 20 per cent which was too high for many idle ponies, whose protein intake must be watched with care if laminitis is to be avoided.

'Horse Coarse Feed Mix'

A newcomer in the late 1970s to the horse nutrition scene. Compounders (manufacturers of animal feeding stuffs which are compounded – mixed) are now mixing up rations of kibbled (coarsely ground) conventional feeding stuffs like oats, barley and nuts, which are mixed with bran and other ingredients to produce a balanced mix with an analysis of 3 per cent oil, 11 per cent protein and 7 per cent fibre. The object of this mix is to offer owners the chance of feeding a traditional type ration without the disadvantages of having to mix it for themselves. Like nuts, one cannot vary the mix for oneself and should a horse have to have its corn cut, then the whole ration must be cut – with home individual mixing one can leave out or increase as the circumstances dictate. Different makes vary.

The only two real advantages over nuts lie in the fact that medicines can be added if required, and it is not finely ground food, so digestion should be normal. Providing the mix comes from a firm of high repute, and the mix is absolutely fresh – never buy in large quantities – then it should provide an alternative to mixing feeds.

Some establishments now have their own rations compounded – but the results I have seen are finely ground and more suited to cattle feeding, than for horses. I personally would never use such a mix for any horses in my care or suggest its use. Finely ground food is dangerous and can cause blockages.

Warning

Should horses and beef cattle be kept on the same premises then *extreme care must be exercised* to ensure that no horses, ponies or donkeys have access to any feeding stuffs containing harmful substances such as monensin sodium, which even in very small quantities can be fatal to horses. A pre-mix used in rations for beef cattle to increase body weight, it has the appearance of fine bran; and if by accident horses should eat even the smallest amount, 5oz (135g) being more than enough to kill, then veterinary help must be obtained without delay. The fatal heart attacks caused by this substance can occur up to three weeks after eating it. It also goes under the name of 'Romensin' and all feed stuffs containing it should be marked on the bags.

5 High-protein Foods

When assessing the protein value of feeding stuffs we must remember that all natural sources of protein will vary, one sample from the next. The protein percentage given in this book is the average and has been supplied by Agricultural Fodder Merchants, or else taken from the labels of bags. The only way to be absolutely sure of any given sample of feeding stuffs is to have it analysed. In this way if your are feeding your own fodder and grain, you can make up an accurate ration. For smaller stables this is not always feasible as they normally have to purchase in smaller amounts. Nevertheless, using the average percentage we can make up our rations to meet the requirements of individual horses according to their work, size and age.

For horses and ponies in light work 10 per cent protein is considered suitable in which case they will have a higher fibre percentage than those doing harder work. A middle of the road ration, 12 per cent, suits many horses that require more protein than the normal ration of 10 per cent, but who, if given the full 14 per cent, will act the fool unless the rider is capable of riding a 'well fed horse'. This last group is for all those doing competition work or sports that require the horse to exert itself over a period of time. To feed less only puts the horse under too great a stress and this in time will lead to the horse breaking down.

Breeding and youngstock require even higher protein owing to the drains nature is making on their system and they must have approximately 15 per cent. If there is too much protein in the ration then, instead of doing good, trouble will ensue. Only feed the amount of protein the horse's system can burn up by means of growing, reproducing, lactating, or just plain hard work and keeping warm in winter.

To raise the normal cereal grain ration from its average of 8·5 per cent protein to one equal to the level required, we must feed a high protein food – foods which if fed with care and in small amounts, can make all the difference to the horse's appearance and well-being. It will be noted that nearly all high protein foods come from the seeds of leguminous plants (seeds within a pod), rather than from cereal grains or grasses that have their seeds encased within a husk.

Linseed

The seed of the flax plant is one of the most useful sources available. Not only being high in protein – 25 per cent – it carries an oil of 12 per cent in a form that the horse can make use of, so that it helps to put flesh on a poor animal and gives the coat a good sheen – a sign of well-being. I am a great believer in linseed and all my horses have had it in winter with very good results. As it contains a poison in its natural state, once soaked, namely prussic acid (hydrocyanic acid, hydrogen cyanide), all linseed must be thoroughly cooked before being fed.

To prepare linseed you will require a large saucepan into which about 4oz (113·4g) of linseed is placed, covered well with water (about halfway up the saucepan) and left to soak overnight. Next day bring to the boil and boil hard for a few minutes to kill off the prussic acid and then simmer for several hours till jellied. A word of *warning*: keep stirring at intervals or else it will catch and burn and, too, watch out for it boiling over; it has a nasty habit of doing so, hence the large saucepan. This quantity of linseed I have found sufficient for one horse for one feed. In this complete jelly form, when cool, it can be mixed with the evening feed or in its hot state in a mash. Another method of using it is to draw off the jelly from the seeds and give it as gruel or linseed tea, the seeds being fed separately or thrown away (wasteful). I normally feed the whole panful as it stands.

A good sample of linseed should be clean, shiny and plump, rather than flat in appearance. Always smell linseed before using it – if rancid, throw away and *never* give to horses.

Soya Bean Meal

The highest source of protein at 45 per cent, with an oil of 6 per cent, soya bean is a very rich feed indeed and only for use on youngstock, breeding stock and horses in very hard work whose riders are capable of coping with a 'fit' horse.

The maximum amount to be fed is 1 lb (0·45 kg). As the meal is made by toasting the ground-up beans, the sample should be of a yellow toasted appearance with a smell characteristic of such a process. River Gipsy was reared on soya bean meal to give her the required protein and the results were very satisfactory. Being high in amino acids it is a perfect grain balancer.

Field Beans

Sometimes called horse beans field beans are small hard beans that in the old days horses had in winter to boost their ration. Not met with so much these days, but with a protein of around the 20 per cent mark they enabled horses to work hard long hours. Dark, reddish brown in colour, horses fed on these beans often earned the term 'full of beans', for they were very fresh. Fed split, and mixed in the corn ration at about the rate of 1 lb (0·45 kg) a day, they are a good source of protein, but rather heating, so must be used with care.

Concentrate Pellets

Formulated for the owner who wishes to feed a cereal type ration but requires a grain balancer concentrate pellets carry a protein tag of 26 per cent, oil 3 per cent, fibre 8.5 per cent. They provide the answer for those who like to feed nuts in their ration, while retaining the old type of feed. Fully vitaminised/mineralised, they can also be used to up the protein of Complete Nuts, but it would be unwise to mix two brands of nuts, for each firm has its own formulas.

Milk Pellets

Carrying a protein of around 23 per cent and an oil of 15·5 per cent according to their make, these small white milk pellets are an excellent source of additional protein being very easily digested. Fed at up to about 1 lb (0·45 kg) a day, horses love them and tiny foals will start eating them at a few days old from one's hand. Unlike other protein supplements, these milk pellets do not hot up a horse, and are therefore safe for all types. Expensive, yes, but for a special purpose worth it. Galavant had them eventing for she could neither take large amounts of cereals, nor would she eat more than a certain amount, and these pellets meant she was getting the oat equivalent she required. She and River Gipsy had them too when River Gipsy was tiny, and I believe it was the milk pellets that saved her life and gave her the strength to overcome her weakness and grow into a strong, well made filly. I have also had excellent results with the tricky problem of feeding a 19-year-old Welsh Cob mare. When fed oats she was too strong for her owner, who wished to hunt, but as fed could neither hold her nor keep flesh on her. I worked out a diet sheet which included milk pellets and within six weeks that mare was well rounded, with a shine on her coat, and her owner happy and once more in control! The mare got her much needed protein and her owner her fun.

Dried Grass Meal or Cubes

As the name implies this is grass that has been dried and then reduced to a powder – either left that way in a meal or made up into cubes. The protein varies in this product, but that made from good grass and lucerne can come out at the high protein levels of over 15 per cent and as such is useful in some diets and to add variety. This meal is, as a rule, the basis of most horse nuts, providing the protein and fibre necessary to bring the feed up to 10 per cent protein and 17 per cent fibre. Naturally there are many other things in horse nuts too, but these figure on most lists one can see.

The foregoing foods are some of the ones available that are safe for the ordinary owner to feed – not always cheap to buy in small quantities but as so little is fed per day in relation to the rest of the ration the cost works out about the same in the long run. There are others one will read about and these will find their way into nuts, but their place is in nuts and not for home use by the ordinary owner.

6 Additional Foods

So far we have dealt with grass, hay, cereal grains and high protein foods, now it is the turn of those foods that play their part in a horse's diet, but which do not readily fit into previous chapters.

Bran

The outer coating of wheat produced during milling flour bran with its protein of 9·5 per cent (though many claim bran has no feed value) and a fibre of 12 per cent is extremely useful in limited quantities.

Though wheat itself is not a suitable grain for horses, as a basis for all cereal grains, and on its own as a mash, bran is a laxative when damp and binding when fed dry.

In the form of a mash it is easily digested by a tired or sick horse. A real mash is cooked in steam, produced from pouring boiling water over it.

The quality of bran varies from large, flat flakes that have masses of flour left in them, down to such fine stuff that, if fed, it would go to a mushy mass inside the horse which would be hard to digest. The very small bran sometimes goes under the heading of miller's offals or wheatings, though in the strict sense of the word these two last named should not be sold as bran.

One can buy straight run bran – all grades together, or broad bran, this being the grade always to aim at buying. In many areas it is hard to buy, but if you buy a new supply having started the previous lot, you should keep going; for one or two horses I never have more than 110¼lb (50kg) in the feed house at any one time. Bran, like other cereal foods, once crushed or milled, has a limited keeping time. Before starting a new sample, or when your current lot has been unused for a little while, smell it carefully – good bran should have a sweet, fresh aroma and be light to handle. Musty, damp bran is useless, dangerous, and should never be fed.

Sugar Beet Pulp and Nuts

These carry a fibre content of 15 per cent (higher than bran) but a sugar content of 22 per cent with protein 18 per cent, so many owners look on sugar beet pulp as their horse's staple diet, their devotion to the stuff being unshakable.

In sensible hands it is perfectly safe, but by its very nature, especially if used in nut form, it can be extremely dangerous. If a person was careless, or children had access to them, they could well be offered to a horse in their dry state and this would choke the horse – *very dangerous* indeed.

In their dry state sugar beet pulp and sugar beet nuts take up only a small space, but when water is added both will swell, requiring a considerable amount of reconstitution as, being dehydrated, they must be thoroughly soaked for 24 hours before being fed. When fully soaked, and to its maximum absorption, the grey looking dehydrated pulp, turns dark having increased its volume by at least treble. If you decide to use either the pulp or the nuts, then the buckets used to soak the stuff must be washed out thoroughly after every soaking; and unused pulp thrown away; it goes sour very quickly and must be fed fresh every day. Having drained off surplus water, the swollen pulp is then mixed into the dry feed containing bran in order to lighten it.

If one's horse is the hungry type or tends to get thin, then sugar beet pulp which, of course, contains sugar might be a useful addition to its feed providing it was only doing ordinary work; if in hard work the pulp would tend to blow the horse out too much and this is where lung and wind damage can occur. Remember though at all times – sugar beet pulp, and above all the nuts, swell with alarming speed and should a horse get hold of any un-soaked or part soaked pulp or nuts, which then would mix with saliva, it could die.

Choppy

Chaff or chopped hay is a very useful lightener and bulk producer for all feeds. The best choppy is produced from seed hay and is made by putting hay (use only good quality hay, never mouldy or dusty hay as some people do) though a special machine called a choppy or chaff cutter. I have a very old hand machine given me many years ago. It has a box into which the hay is laid to pass through the cutters. Hand powered, it is good exercise but power driven models are available. When not in use, tie the handle and cover the blade with a sack to prevent accidents. Incidentally, chaff in this respect does not refer to the chaff from corn thrashing – this is the cavings and useless as a feed. Besides seed hay, hard meadow hay can be used, and also good quality oat straw, but I prefer seed hay, as the value of the feed then retains its protein level. For those unable to cut their own choppy, there are now mixtures of hay and straw chaff containing molasses; of these, Mollichaff is the best known. Beware of poor grade substitutes.

Black Treacle

Molasses or black treacle, is an excellent source of sugar having a content of 37·8 per cent. Its value lies in the fact that it supplies energy in the form of sugar, plus making the feeds palatable, with a reduction in the risk of dust. Feed in small quantities – mix 1 teaspoonful of treacle (bought from the grocer or in bulk from a corn merchant when it is called molasses) in ½pt (250cc) of warm water, pour over the dry feed and mix in.

Molassine Meal

A fibrous dark brown meal with a sugar content of 38 per cent and fibre of 5·5 per cent. Produced from the residue of extracting treacle or molasses from the cane it is used for the same reasons as liquid molasses, but the feed has to be damped with warm water after mixing the meal into the feed in the normal way. When buying molassine meal make sure the sample is fresh, it can go rancid and then will poison; and, it has been known for it to be mixed up with bulb fibre; should anyone try this trick on, feel the meal and smell it, the true stuff is sticky and sweet smelling, and has no connection whatsoever with the fibre.

Carrots

A root vegetable much enjoyed by horses and rich in vitamins. Unwashed carrots are best as they keep better and have more taste. The unwashed carrots must be scrubbed before being cut into *lengths* (never rounds which could choke the horse); or peeled so the horse gets the peel and the owner can eat the centre part. Horses love carrots and they help to prevent the blood overheating – feed about 1 lb (0·45 kg) a day.

Potatoes

These can be fed cooked, but must be scrubbed first. Or else clean potato peels can be boiled up instead. A useful means of extra nourishment in bad weather for horses on ordinary work; drain off and feed the soft potatoes or peels mushed up and lightened with bran. Being full of starch they provide an oat = potato ratio of 1:3·5. I used potato peel on two of my horses after the Second World War when food was still rationed and in short supply. It helps to keep flesh on the type that loses it in winter, 2 lb (0·90 kg) a day is enough, and it is best fed at night to allow for complete digestion. To be used when other food is hard to come by.

Fig. 1 Open shed suitable for storing hay and straw

Fig. 2 Choppy (chaff) – made from rye grass hay by passing through a hand-powered choppy cutter

Fig. 3 Empty haynet well clear of the floor – Galavant 12 yrs 7 mths

Fig. 4 Droppings from a healthy corn fed horse

Fig. 5 Haynet lashed to a tree, River Gypsy, 1 yr 8 mths

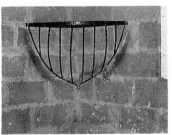

Fig. 6 Wall mounted corner hay rack

Fig. 7 5-gallon water carrier (22.71 l)

Fig. 8 Wide bottomed metal water bucket. 4-gallon size (18.71 l)

Fig. 9 8-gallon feeding bowl, useful for youngstock (36.34 l)

Fig. 10 Wide bottomed plastic water or feeding bucket. 4-gallon (18.71 l)

Fig. 11 Fixed bucket holder, potentially dangerous

Fig. 12 Automatic indoor water bowl

Fig. 13 Galavant the Sunday after her arrival

Fig. 14 A month later she was beginning to show real improvement

Fig. 15 A year after her arrival Galavant was in fine condition

Fig. 16 Galavant, 13 yrs 8 mths, nine months in foal

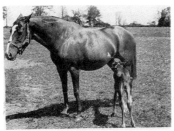

Fig. 17 Now feeding a foal, River Gipsy, 2 days old

Fig. 18 Investigating the mare's supply of concentrates – River Gipsy, 3 days old

Fig. 19 At 5 days old, River Gypsy was eating too

Fig. 20 Galavant and River Gipsy by River Poaching, 1 week old

Fig. 21 At 4 weeks old River Gipsy was eating her share

Fig. 22 By 6 weeks she was looking a different foal

Fig. 23 River Gipsy, at 9 months – note round cornered water trough

Fig. 24 River Gypsy with mid-day feed aged 1 yr 11 mths – note the 'Rockie' on the fence

7 Vitamins and Minerals

Vitamins and minerals are essential for every horse to enable its body to function correctly. Owing to modern farming methods, land and feeding stuffs tend today to be less proficient in these commodities than in the old days. This is partly due to the dressing and spraying of land with chemicals which tend to trap minerals in the ground; and to harvesting methods the crop was sun dried in the old days but is now replaced by a hot air drier in a barn, which is hardly conducive to the production of good vitamin supplies. Hence the necessity to provide additional sources of both vitamins and minerals, together with trace-elements.

Before going further into the different vitamins and minerals, their functions and natural sources needs to be described.

Vitamins fall into two categories: fat-soluble and water-soluble. The A, D, and E groups belong to the fat-soluble category. This means that any taken in excess of immediate requirements are stored in the liver and fat depôts, for release at a future time; in other words if the horse takes in more than required in the summer months, it can use them up during the winter when their supply is limited.

Vitamins of the B, C, and K groups are water-soluble and cannot be stored in the body against future needs so must be supplied daily.

Minerals, including trace-elements (those required in very small amounts, but still vital to the horse's well being), are necessary both to build up and maintain bone and ensure mineral balance in the bloodstream.

So much for the many different vitamins and minerals required by a horse if it is to be maintained in good health.

Figure 7.1 VITAMINS

Group	Name	Function	Source
A	Carotene	Growth and well-being of all horses, especially youngsters. Vision: Protects mucous membrane: Maintains tone of respiratory organs: Helps resistance to disease.	Present in green foods, fish oils, and carrots. Can be stored in the liver.
B_1	Aneurin Thiamin(e)	Release of energy from carbohydrates: Healthy nerves. Lack causes stunted growth and neuritis.	Water soluble, found in yeast and liver. To some extent in wheat bran and untreated cereals.
B_2 Complex	Riboflavin	Energy release: lack of, can cause sores and cracks in mouth.	
	Nicotinic acid (Niacin) Pantothenic acid	Lack of, causes internal upsets and disorders, mental confusion. Associated with skin health and growth.	
	Choline	Prevents fats accumulating in the liver. Connected with inter-action with amino-acids.	
	Biotin	Formerly known as vitamin H.	
B_6	Pyridoxine	Concerned with skin: healthy nervous system: blood cell formation and metabolism of fats.	
B_{12}	Cyan-ocobalamin	Required for growth; Helps the health of the nerve cells; and to prevent anaemia, especially after stress, or antibiotic treatment.	
	Folic acid	Now found to be of importance to horses.	Green foods.
	Folinic acid Inositol		
C	Ascorbic acid	Required to maintain general health. Heal and repair damaged tissue, and ward off disease.	Present in fruit juices and root vegetables; green foods.
D D_1 D_2 D_3	Radiostol or Irradiated ergosterol	Sunshine vitamin produced by the sun's rays on the horse's skin. Associated with Vitamin A in fish oils and is necessary for bone and teeth formation.	Sunlight: Cod liver oil: (never feed it rancid, as it is then poisonous). Halibut Liver Oil.

44

E	d-alapha-Tocopheryl Acetate	Anti-sterility factor: Prevents muscular atrophy by maintaining good muscle cell function in skeletal and heart muscles; aids build up of muscles in growing foals.	Fat-soluble: Found in wheat germ and green foods, cereals and many of the oil cakes. Milk. Destroyed by Proprionic Acid.
H		Now known as Biotin.	
K		Of importance to blood.	Fat soluble, present in Alpha, green foods, soya bean and fish meals.

Under normal conditions the horse should receive sufficient vitamin/mineral requirements from its food, if of high quality, but as it is impossible to be sure that one's horse is receiving an adequate level of all the different vitamins and minerals, it is wise to supply an additional source in some form or other.

Vitamin/mineral supplements come in many different forms – powder, fine meal, liquid, pellets, crumbs, blocks, licks, or mixed into either ordinary horse nuts or concentrate and milk pellets. Some are straight vitamin/mineral supplements, others contain honey, cod liver oil or linseed – the list is endless and no doubt will be increased even more in years to come.

Which supplement to choose depends largely on one's own horse, how it is fed and the work it is doing. Some supplements have a comprehensive range of vitamins and minerals and are aimed at providing a full range for the horse to draw on, presuming that it is already receiving a certain amount, but not all from its normal diet.

Not all supplements have a comprehensive range, some only cover the more usual vitamins and minerals, but I feel if one is going to supplement, then one might as well make a job of it. Of the different brands on the market, one must just pick the one most suited to your horse. The price varies considerably, but the most expensive is not always the best – choose the brand by its value, rather than its price tag. If in any doubt as to the most suitable brand to choose, consult your veterinary surgeon – he knows your horse and is the best person to advise you, for should your horse have some form of deficiency, such as an iron deficiency, then the horse would probably require one of the

Figure 7.2   MINERALS (including trace-elements)

Name	Function	Source
Calcium (Ca)	Necessary for strong bone formation; teeth, muscle function and blood.	Minerals are inorganic elements which are present in the soil, and through the soil in plant life; some soils, and therefore plant life is better provided with minerals than others.
Phosphorus (P)	Balances the calcium in the bone structure; repair of tissue following strenuous work.	
Magnesium (Mg)	Required for skeletal development and muscular tone.	
Iron (Fe)	Important in the formation of haemoglobin, the means by which oxygen is absorbed by the blood. Lack of it causes different forms of anaemia.	
Copper (Cu)	Necessary in conjunction with iron.	
Manganese (Mn)	Is required for bone structure and reproduction.	
Iodine (I)	Essential for the full functioning of the thyroid gland, and ensures balanced glandular functions.	
Cobalt (Co)	Helps the animal to synthetise Vitamin B_{12}.	
Potassium	Influences metabolism of carbohydrates and is incorporated in the red blood corpuscles and cells of muscles.	
Sodium Chloride (NaCl)	Common salt, without which no horse can do well as it is essential for body fluids and blood levels. Lack of it causes cramp.	
Sulphur Nickel Zinc		
Selenium	Closely involved with the activity of Vitamin E. Excess can lead to Selenium Toxicity, more common in dry areas where grass is sparse. 'Alkali Disease' – loss of hair on mane and tail, lameness, bone lesions, including twisted legs in foals. Sloughing off of hooves. A trace-element that is essential, but in the correct form and quantity.	

tonic type supplements formulated to cope with the lack of iron, and only obtainable through a veterinary surgeon; an ordinary supplement in these cases would be insufficient.

Never feed more than one brand of supplement at any one

time. If you do, then you could well cause an imbalance, which is as serious as not giving one at all and causing a deficiency. Use your commonsense, and never over-dose; if anything under-dose slightly, especially if the horse is already getting some vitamins and minerals from its usual nuts.

Horses on concentrate pellets and milk pellets at their full rate will not require additional supplements under normal conditions though a veterinary surgeon may advise some form of additional vitamins or minerals in special cases. Most horses on ordinary nuts and not on a cereal straight ration, should be receiving an adequate supply as they are fully vitaminised and mineralised, though not (so I gather from reading their formula) to the same extent as a comprehensive supplement; their range is more equal to some of the smaller range supplements covering the essential ones.

The possible exception being 'Thrive' – an imported product containing Montmorillonite – derived from Sodium Bentonite, mined in Queensland, Australia, which aids digestion of grain-fed horses and has a marked calming effect. A mineral supplement it can be fed in conjunction with a vitamin/mineral one.

Though all supplements carry a coverage of calcium/phosphorus combination in their make-up, it may still be necessary to use a grain balancer. All cereals are in fact low in calcium in relation to phosphorus – bran and maize having the worst ratio, and oats, barley, linseed, soya bean meal and field beans all having a very definite difference in the ratio of calcium to phosphorus, which to be correct should be balanced. To correct this calcium deficiency in these foods it is necessary to add pure calcium to the horse's ration in some form or other. Natural sources such as hay – lucerne being very high in calcium – are not always available in the quantities required, so use has to be made of such products as bone flour. This is specially treated bones, ground to a fine powder and passed suitable for animal feeding. For a long time this was the accepted form in which additional calcium was given. Providing the sample is pure and fresh, it is safe, but it has a nasty habit of going bad and could cause trouble. Pure ground chalk will also provide calcium, but nowadays ground limestone is used in preference by many veterinary surgeons.

Ground limestone is a fine grey coloured powder, which when freshly ground has an oily smell about it. Introduced slowly into a ration at 1 oz per 10 lb (28·37 g per 4·53 kg) of cereals a day, it will soon be accepted by the horse. Sometimes in very special cases this dose will be increased by your veterinary surgeon. With Galavant, as she was very calcium deficient following her past treatment, we had to double the dose – she had been receiving ½ oz (28·37 g) a day on a 5 lb (2·26 kg) ration and she was put onto 1 oz (14·17 g) but never do this without first asking – too much calcium is as dangerous as too little. A true balance must be struck. Carrying a calcium of 97 per cent is a top-class sample – my new supply had this figure, it may have one lower. So, enquire from your supplier what percentage of calcium the ground limestone in question has been given.

Now obtaining this ground limestone can be a problem. Recently Bailey's have started marketing it, but it is absolutely essential to obtain the limestone as supplied to the animal feeding stuffs industry, any other type of ground limestone would be highly dangerous. Ask your Veterinary Surgeon before using Boneflour or Ground Limestone in conjunction with 'Thrive', as this has a high calcium content in its own right.

Cod Liver Oil

In its pure form it can be added to the feed of young horses and others in need of additional vitamin D, or a combination of vitamins A and D, of which it is a rich natural source. Vitamin E is also present but not in the same extent. For growing youngstock it is invaluable; as River Gipsy had been receiving both her vitamin/mineral supplement and ground limestone, she had not had the addition of cod liver oil, but early in 1978 she developed periostitis and became very lame – an inflammation of the surface of the bone affecting the periosteum (membrane surrounding the bone). Rest and additional vitamin D was the answer in her case and now her legs are grand – at long last straight. A wine glassful a day is the usual dose for an adult horse and half a glass for a foal, unless your veterinary surgeon tells you otherwise. I only use cod liver oil on veterinary advice as it is one of those useful additions to the feed in time of need; though throughout the winter youngstock do benefit from it. Pour onto the mixed feed and stir well in, washing out the glass measure afterwards to prevent it going rancid.

Salt

Common salt can either be bought from the grocer or from your merchant according to the number of horses you have to feed. Every horse requires 1 oz (28·35 g) per day – I mix ½ oz (14·17 g) into two feeds a day, otherwise the feed could be too salty for some horses.

Salt Licks

For horses out at grass the best way to supply salt is in the form of a lick. There are various sorts on the market, but Rockies are the most useful as they do not wash away and contain, besides salt, magnesium, iodine, iron, cobalt, manganese, zinc all in chelated form (to quote *Black's Veterinary Dictionary*, 'they are substances which have the property of binding divalent metal ions to form stable, soluble complexes which are non-ionised and so virtually lacking in toxicity fo the metal concerned') so that the horse does get access to these while at grass if not receiving a ration containing them. They can be fastened to a fence by a plaited piece of nylon binder twine. Note the knot needs to be fixed by a staple driven home tight; failure to hold the knot, should it come undone, the weight, 22 lb (10 kg), might cause serious injury to the horse. Alternatively, the salt lick can be placed on the ground in a convenient spot.

In the stable a smaller block can be provided in a special holder placed so as to avoid the risk of the horse knocking into it. Some now contain Selenium, a safe way to provide this trace element.

In recent years there has been a revived interest in using centuries-old known sources of vitamins and minerals, and their trace elements found in nature through herbs and plants.

For this reason I am here including the best known, as I feel in a book of this kind they are necessary to give the reader as full a knowledge as is possible.

Seaweed-Kelp/Norwegian Kelp

Kelp, a large seaweed of the algae family, is an extensive source of a vast range of vitamins, minerals and amino-acids. Use only mixes from reputable firms; Maxicrop International are to the forefront in the field and also produce a liquid dressing for pasture land, an excellent way to improve the quality of the grazing.

Comfrey

The only known land plant capable of extracting vitamin B_{12} from the soil, comfrey is a rich source of vitamins, including vitamin C, amino-acids and potassium often deficient in the diets of high-performance horses. In addition it is a source of easily absorbed organic calcium. A herb known since the days of the ancient Greeks for its powers of healing, internally and externally, which maybe is due to the fact that it also contains allantoin and cholin in its make-up.

Garlic

Noted as a counter-reactionary to dust allergies and other respiratory problems, garlic is recommended by herbalists for clearing mucus from the back of the throat and nose that leads to coughing. Also clears cholesterol from the blood, keeping it clear and free-flowing. Helps laminitis, sweet-itch (though this may be because the skin of a garlic-fed horse smells and flies are not keen) and rheumatism. Garlic contains vitamins A, B_1, B_2, B_3, and C, minerals, trace elements, essential oils which contain sulphur and a substance called crontonaldehyde.

Cider Vinegar

Produced from apples, cider vinegar is rich in vitamins and minerals, especially potassium. An old-time coat conditioner and muscle toner.

Nettles

They contain iron, protein and vitamins A and C, plus minerals.

Dandelion

Vitamins B and C plus potassium.

Rose Hips

Vitamins C, E, and B group, folic acid and biotin. Vitamin C being especially high.

Fenugreek

Of the leguminous family, with a feed value akin to linseed, fenugreek contains oil and protein. A good tonic rich in vitamins including E.

Yeast/Brewers' Yeast

High in the B vitamins and a rich source of biotin. *Living yeast* should *never* be fed to horses, they cannot absorb it in that form, which could cause excessive harm. It must be *inactive* yeast, which is said to have calming effect on nervous horses.

Remember though, if you decide to use a 'Natural' supplement, then choose very carefully from a reputable source and abide by their instructions. In this day and age of pesticides and fertilisers, plants growing in the wild can be dangerous if, unknown to you, they have been 'treated'. Also, in the case of seaweed, if growing in or gathered from an area that came under the effects of the radiation cloud from Chernobyl in April 1986, being an algae, it could still be contaminated – as is the lichen that reindeer live off of in Scandinavia. So buy from a reputable firm who will ensure only safe products are used.

Remember, herbs have many other qualities, some even a 'two way' effect – in tiny quantities they are good, in the wrong dosage the result could mean you are in real trouble. Also, if your horse is going to be subject to 'dope' testing, check before using a product, to ensure that it will pass without question any random test. This also applies to all supplements, not just 'Natural' ones.

8 Preparing Feeds

The secret of sound feeding lies with the preparation of feeds – it is one thing to scoop up a quantity of various foods, chuck them in a bucket, slap in the odd supplement, splash on some water, and throw the result haphazardly into a manger or feed tin as the case may be. But, it is quite another matter to weigh out accurately each different foodstuff in the ration, place them in a clean bucket, mix together carefully prior to damping thoroughly, and then tipping it with care in the manger, giving an extra stir round if required. The former method normally leads to bad feeders and consequently poor doers; whereas the latter method gives one the satisfaction of having a fit, healthy, contented horse in the stable or paddock that makes the most of its food, and is a credit to own.

Mixed Feeds

These are the traditional type of feeds where the various foods to be used are mixed-up freshly for each feed. Some big establishments mix-up enough for a whole day in a big barrow and then dole out so much per horse, very often with a shovel. This to my mind is no way to feed a horse, each *must* be fed individually – no two horses are the same and even two on the same ration may like their food mixed differently in order to get the best results out of that feed by that particular horse. To mix in bulk for a whole day prevents the food from having that fresh smell and taste, so essential for sound feeding and willing eaters.

What one can do though to save time, or if the regular feeder is going to be away for the next feed or two, is to weigh out all the dry ingredients into a clean, dry, 4 gallon (18·17l) bucket, preferably leaving out the various supplements to be added just before the final mixing and preparation. Horses are fussy feeders and can be put off by different smells and tastes, and two supplements can act on one another to change the flavour (salt for instance draws damp and could make a fine powder supplement damp just by being next to it, and once damp this could affect the taste of that supplement, so it is far safer to include it just before feeding). It is small details like this that can make all the difference to a horse clearing its food with enjoyment, or else picking at it. Sour feeds are unappetising, and only a few horses will eat them when proffered, the others so often get termed 'not hungry'. They are hungry all right, but will rather starve than eat badly prepared feeds.

Preparing a good mixed feed requires a little time – time well spent if the horse benefits from it. A clean bucket is essential, a dirty one will merely taint the food. In to the bucket food is weighed – some people use a measure though this method may be quicker but is not accurate and the horse will never do as well as one who has its food weighed for each feed. In order to weigh out the food one must have some form of scales.

I place the given amount of bran in first, followed by oats, and any other cereal food, like flaked maize or soya bean meal. If nuts form part of the ration, these follow and the whole is topped off by handfuls of choppy. The feed is now ready for the inclusion of any dry supplements like salt, ground limestone and vitamins/minerals. By putting them in last you can ensure none are forgotten, for some are only included in certain feeds and, too, as they tend to work down through the other layers they will come to a halt in the bran and not get wasted by sticking to the bucket. Should oats or choppy have formed the bottom layer the fine ingredients would go straight through and be partly wasted.

Next, mix all these things thoroughly together and pour over the whole a measureful of warm water and, if used, black treacle. Mix thoroughly again till the whole is evenly damp – neither too wet nor too dry, but just so that the whole comes up light and fluffy with a pleasing, appetising aroma. There is nothing beastlier than a soggy wet feed, that turns sour before the horse has had time to face up to eating it all – feeds mixed with warm water remain palatable for considerably longer than those mixed with cold water. Rather than go soggy, they tend to dry out. Damping feeds has two objects – to prevent dust being breathed in while feeding, and to ensure proper mastication and therefore digestion. Also, they cannot separate their favourite bits out so easily. Liquids like cod liver oil are added after mixing and stirred in, while carrots go in last of all – they have a nasty habit of sending a sharp sliver up under one's finger nail if put in before all mixing has been completed!

Feeds for Sick Horses

These feeds must be very tempting; many people just give hay, but this to my mind is wrong. To deprive a horse of its feed just because it is sick or injured is, unless they are refusing it of their own free will, or really should be starved, illogical, for on top of pain they will be fretting. To overcome the situation I give 'false feeds' that is a similar feed to normal, minus just the cereal or concentrates, adding, to make up the difference, extra choppy and carrots and anything else that may take their fancy – cooked linseed, boiled barley or oats, glucose if they like it. There are many ways one can vary the food and make it palatable. Above all horses require their vitamins and minerals if they are to heal and mend properly or recover their strength. Providing the feed is easily digested and not heating up the horse it can only do good.

Mashes

Soft feed mashes, made up on a basis of bran are easily digested. They are useful for tired horses on return from work, for sick or injured horses to keep their bowels working correctly while they are standing idle in the stable and, once a week, useful in reducing the load on the digestive system before a day's rest.

There are various types of mashes, the best known being a Bran mash which is made by placing between 1½lb (0·68kg) and 3lb (1·36kg) of broad bran in a bucket, 4 gallon (18·17l) type according to the size of the horse – a pony will require the smaller amount, a large horse the full 3lb (1·36kg). Next, mix in a handful, 1oz (28·35g) of salt, and then pour a large kettle of really boiling water over the whole and stir thoroughly. The bran should be wet but not soggy; satisfied the bran is of the right consistency, next cover the top of the bucket with either a folded clean hessian sack, a piece of clean blanket over a towel or stable rubber or something clean that will hold in the heat, for now the mash has to stand for at least an hour to steam itself and make properly. Once one can move one's own bare hand about in the bran without burning, then the mash is ready to give to the horse. If the horse is allowed corn, then a handful of oats or oats and flaked maize is a welcome addition and will encourage those that refuse mashes to eat up. I also put in the vitamins and minerals as I like my horses to have these at the correct feed times.

Mashes should be given at night and to a horse not worked the next day, or only given walking exercise for a short while – they act as a purgative. Some people mix Epsom salts into a mash before a rest day – I never do and never have had cause to do so. If your horse is correctly fed then it should not require such severe treatment, the only exception to my refusal to give Epsom salts would be if my veterinary surgeon advised it for some specific case, but to do it every Saturday night and Christmas Eve to save exercising your horse the next day is all wrong!

Linseed Mashes

Made with linseed that has been soaked and cooked as already described and the mixed into the bran before the boiling water is poured over – less boiling water will be required as the boiling linseed will have replaced a certain amount of it. Cover and leave to cool in the same way. More nourishing and most welcome by a tired or sick horse who is allowed protein.

Pudding Mash

Some people believe in boiling up together in a copper oats, barley, linseed and possibly maize; then mixing the resulting mass of stodge with bran to form what they term a 'mash', but which is nothing like a true mash. It resembles a 'pudding' that is heavy and solid. This mixture is then shovelled up off the floor or from a trough, dumped in a bucket and transported to its unfortunate recipient, still exhausted from a long, hard day's hunting. No horse can digest such a feed, and having had to look after horses fed in this manner for a while, I know how it is just not properly digested – small wonder horses receiving this type of diet have staring, harsh coats and hollow flanks.

Gruels

Gruels are made from mixing about a double handful of coarse oatmeal (the kind sold at a grocers for making true porridge), with cold water and then stirring well. When thoroughly mixed pour on more boiling water to bring the quantity up to the required amount; allow to cool to blood heat and offer to the horse.

Easily digested, a gruel must be thin enough for the horse to drink. It is used for tired horses coming in from hard work and long hours out of the stable with no food; and for horses that are either ill, or convalescing from a debilitating disease or injury. Milk can be substituted for part of the water if a more nourishing drink is required and either salt or sugar added if desired.

Linseed Tea

This has the same function as gruel, being acceptable for tired or sick horses, and is made by drawing off the jelly part of boiled linseed (prepared in the same way as for ordinary linseed jelly, but using more water to make it thinner), which, once cool, is thinned and offered to the horse to drink.

Straight Nuts and Straight Oats

If one is feeding either nuts or oats on their own without any additional foods mixed in with them, then just weigh out the correct amount and give to the horse. With nuts this is often the usual way, but remember nuts are dry and the horse will drink more water when on a diet of just nuts. Also, if you feed a horse a ration of nuts first thing in the morning on an empty stomach and then turn it out to grass which has a lot of dew or moisture in it, the wet grass will act on the nuts in the horse's stomach and cause serious trouble. It is far safer to mix nuts with either chaff or chaff and bran as this prevents the chewed up nuts becoming a stodgy mass which is hard to digest and merely swells in the stomach. Straight oats are best mixed with chaff or chaff and some bran to ensure that the horse chews properly. In small quantities they are perfectly safe to feed on their own.

Regardless of what or how we feed our horses, the state and colour of their droppings is the surest indication of whether we are feeding correctly. A healthy horse that is stabled and on a diet of seed hay and a mixed feed will have droppings of a light brown colour that are well formed but break on hitting the ground. A horse receiving a lot of grass in some form or other will have greenish droppings, and this applies to horses on the high fibre low protein nuts. Quantities of undigested food should not be evident, though some oats may be, their number though is few in reality. Digestion is the key to sound feeding.

9 Feeding for Fitness and Health

In the preceding chapters we have investigated the whys and wherefores of feeding and the different types of foods and how to prepare them. Now it is time to see how best to feed horses in order to ensure that they are fit and healthy, and able to gain the maximum amount of benefit out of their food.

In the first chapter we dealt with the basic principles of sound feeding, and the overall amounts of food required by a horse according to its size and weight. Now we have to decide how best to proportion the various feeding stuffs at our disposal, so as to meet the special requirements of each individual horse in our care.

Roughage or Bulk Foods

Roughage is the basic of every horse's diet. In general, during the summer months of May, June, July and possibly August, with September depending on the weather and growth of grass, horses will require only good, clean grass together with a supply of fresh, clean water, and adequate shade to meet their daily needs when not working, or in light work. In winter, when the grass loses its feeding value, they will require additional food to maintain their level of nourishment and to stoke up their internal central heating system which helps them ward off the cold weather.

As the growing stage of grass fades with the onset of the autumn, the sap in the grass stems starts to recede. By winter the grass is no longer green and fades to a brown colour not unlike poor hay. This is dead grass, for that is what it is once it has flowered, and has little or no feeding value in it, beyond providing some rather coarse roughage or fibre intake.

In summer when it is very dry, grass will also turn brown, but as the sap was running at the time the sun dried the grass up, it is more likely to have some nourishment in it – though if the grass had already flowered, then that grass would have been verging on dying, so the feed value would have diminished anyway; nevertheless horses under such dry conditions will require additional food either in the form of proper hay or concentrates – or both, according to their overall condition and desire for food. Extra water will be required as well to compensate for the lack of moisture in the grass. Horses often prefer grass to other foods when it is fresh and succulent, so if they will eat 'dry' food in summer they normally require it. Beware though of the greedy feeders who will eat anything and everything in sight – these must be restricted or else they will make themselves over-fat and ill.

Prolonged drought means all the food value has been burnt right out of the grass, and when this happens winter feeding must commence forthwith. It was very noticeable during the summer of 1976 how uneasy all the animals became – moos, baas, whinnies, the countryside rang with them from early in the morning to late into the night. Galavant, normally content with her summer routine of in by day away from the flies and out at night, became increasingly reluctant to stay in the burnt up field, even with extra food and water always available; no doubt she had memories of her past – they never forget.

Coping with excessively wet weather is just as much a problem. This, too, will affect grazing, as the grass becomes waterlogged, and once this has occurred, the food value recedes owing to the excessive water intake being too great for the amount of nourishment present – it is like mixing water with a carton of double cream, it just becomes rather watery milk. To rectify this, dry matter must be fed to mop up the excess water and balance the soft over-wet grass in the horse's stomach. Hay, or hay together with an energy food of the mixed feed variety is the most suitable; *but* on *no* account feed straight nuts – nuts on their own under these conditions could prove fatal, especially if the horse was kept in the stable over night, given a feed of nuts in the morning and then turned out on such grass. Waterlogged grass can often cause diarrhoea if the horse does not receive sufficient dry matter to act as a binding agent in the horse's intestine. Continued diarrhoea has a very lowering effect on the horse's health, and should be rectified with all speed.

Diarrhoea is at any time serious, as it is an indication that all is not well with the horse's digestion; the causes of which can be varied – poison, illness, incorrect feeding – these are but three causes, so call your veterinary surgeon if the symptoms do not clear up within 24 hours.

If your horse has a temperature as well, telephone for advice immediately. Incidentally, should you notice an unaccustomed smell either from the horse's breath or from the diarrhoea, then tell the vet. This smell is often one of the first indications as to the cause of an illness and could prove a vital clue. It is far better to call in help either too soon or even unnecessarily, than leave it and have a dead horse – with poisoning and severe illnesses time and speed are the essence of recovery.

Feeding Hay

This can be carried out in three ways: loose on the ground, in racks, or in hay nets. This applies to horses whether at grass, stabled or yarded.

Whichever method you adopt the hay must first be shaken up thoroughly to ensure foreign objects are removed and mouldy patches are not lurking in the folds of the bale. At baling time it is quite amazing the variety of things that can be picked up – glass, stones, branches, bits of metal from the hay-making equipment. We once even had an open penknife fall out of a bale several months after baling – in fact it was this knife that made me so careful over shaking up hay for although a great number of bales were opened and searched at the time, it turned up open. It did no damage, but the result could have been very serious.

Regardless of how it is fed all hay must be weighed before each feed if an accurate amount is going to be given. If fed loose, the hay can either be placed against the wall of the box in a spot where the horse is not likely to mix it with droppings or stale on it (this will ruin the hay for feeding), or else on the ground in the field. If outside, then in the corner of a clean shed is best, or else out in the middle of the field on a bit of dry land, should there be several horses being fed at once – otherwise a kicking and biting match can ensue. For this reason always put down one extra pile to the number of horses being fed. On the other hand, if you just have one horse, or a mare and foal used to sharing the same food, it can be placed against the fence in a sheltered spot.

Hay racks are another alternative to loose hay. In the field, large racks (normally on legs) made of wood are used, though metal ones in different shapes are used on farms. These racks hold one or more bales of hay at a time, and should have lids on to keep the hay dry, otherwise it gets wet and goes nasty. They keep the hay off the ground, but unless on hard standing or in a dry field or yard, they tend to get very poached (deep, holding mud) around the rack where the horses stand to feed.

Foals though with the high racks would have a problem to reach the hay, a problem that arises with indoor racks. There are two types normally used – the wall type that either fastens into a corner, or along the wall; and the corner type that is boxed in like a deep manger having either a solid or slatted bottom. The wall type is high enough to be safe (they should be at least the height of an average human from the ground), is out of reach of a foal, and should they try their eyes, ears and nostrils will get full of hayseeds and dust, a problem that arises with mature horses if the rack is high enough to be really clear of the danger of a caught foot, should the horse roll beneath it. One winter a friend's hunter did just this one night and was found on her back in the morning with a hoof firmly caught between the rungs. Mercifully, the groom who found her acted swiftly and managed somehow to free the foot without damage.

Boxed-in floor racks let the horse reach the hay more easily, and are much simpler to fill, the feeder does not get a faceful every time the rack is filled, as can happen with the high type, but the hayseeds collect along with the dust for the horse to inhale as it eats, constituting another hazard to the horse's health. Being deep, should a horse put a hoof into this type of rack, the result could be serious. The similar design of mangers are shallower and therefore easier to release the horse. One mare I knew was forever putting one or both her forefeet into her manger where she would wait, jacked up in front till rescued! Had it been a deep hay rack the story would have been different.

This now brings us to the last and most common method of feeding hay – hay nets. If a net is correctly tied (so that when empty it cannot hang down near the floor for the horse to get its foot caught) then it should be as safe as any other means of feeding and a great deal less wasteful. It must be properly filled – open the neck wide and, holding with one hand, stuff it full with the other. When ready hang by the draw rope from a 'spring balance' to weigh, if over-full, take some out. If not up to weight for that particular net, stuff more in until the correct weight is achieved. This weighing saves a vast amount of hay over the year and ensures the horse is receiving the correct ration; even when on an 'ad lib' hay ration it is essential to know how much is being eaten.

A normal net holds from 8 to 12 lb (3·62 to 5·44 kg) of seed hay, less of meadow as it is bulkier, and once full should be hung at least 6 ft (1·82 m) from the floor. Pass the free end of the doubled rope that draws the top together, through the ring on the wall, pull the net up as tight to the ring as it will go, hold it there with one hand and pass the end through the net, fairly near the bottom, pull up really tight again and then tie with a quick release knot onto the net itself – never on the ring as the latter lets the net drop when empty. Once tied like this the net should not become a hazard, but if a horse did catch a foot in the mesh, then they can be cut down swiftly. Nets out in the field must be firmly secured to an upright of the fence by lashing the net to the post – pass the rope from side to side over the post, taking up a loop of net from each side and then fastening as before, this will prevent the net shifting or sagging when empty. If you have a tree or a shed with a ring in it, or on the outside, then fasten the net to the ring in the same way as in a box, this is far safer than on the fence. Incidentally, young foals should not be fed hay from a net but have all their hay loose on the ground until they are old enough not to put their hoofs in the mesh of the net by pawing. River Gipsy was taught to eat from a net when young but only when I was with her, removing the mud from her and Galavant in the garage to prevent the hay and straw in their box becoming dusty and muddy.

Never use those vast nets designed for two or three horses. They are dangerous as it is impossible to hang them high enough, or when really full, to lift them far from the floor. Far safer to use two nets, this should be enough for most horses on a full ration and if on a small ration, then they will require three nets a day to compensate for the lack of concentrates. Remember that 10lb (4·53 kg) of seed hay requires 12lb (5·44 kg) of meadow hay to replace it value for value. Hay such as ryegrass, or ryegrass mixture has a greater feeding value than if I was feeding meadow hay. For this reason it often works out no more expensive in the long run to feed seed hay than it does meadow, though normally the seed hay is the more expensive.

When working out your ration you must adjust the amounts according to the grade and type of hay used – that cut early before flowering is far more nutritious than that which is made from grass that has flowered; seed hay is normally cut early, whereas meadow hay tends to be left to get more 'bottom' (the underneath part), rendering the crop of less value from the feed point of view than if it had been cut with the sap still running, though of course the late cut gives a heavier crop and makes up into a greater number of bales! If you are making your own hay try, weather pemitting, to cut at the correct time, rather than waiting till you have a heavier crop. It is far better to have a good light crop, than a heavy one of poor quality hay. Meadow hay cut early and well made can often be evalued on the same basis as seed hay, whereas seed hay cut late after the sap has started to recede, will end up ranking with second grade hay and be of little use to horses owing to the coarse fibre content and lack of protein. So choose your hay carefully and buy the best you can find – some years are easier than others. With *HorseHage* and similar types the amount required will be less to give the same value.

Energy and High Protein Foods

We 'stoke our horse's internal engine' to produce energy which enables it to carry out work without undue fatigue or stress. These foods are rather like fuel for a car engine, the better the quality the greater the power or energy generated (in the case of the horse, the greater the quality) and the greater percentage of protein in the food, the greater the food value.

No one would dream of running a small car on fuel designed for racing cars, it would in all probability explode; so in the same way it is very wrong to feed high protein foods, designed for horses doing hard work like racing and three-day eventing, to a small child's pony – it too would probably explode and certainly become ill from a too-rich diet. On the other hand a horse being asked to perform at speed and work really hard cannot possibly achieve its full potential if it is deprived of sufficient protein to maintain and repair muscle tissue.

Figure 9.1   CHOOSING THE CORRECT FOOD

Feeding stuff	Protein	Oil	Fibre	Sugar	Cal.	Phosp.
Oats	8·5%	4%	9%	–	Low	High
Barley	8·5%	3·5%	9·5%	–	L	H
Flaked maize	8·5%–9%	4·5%	4·5%	–	L*	H
Bran	9·5%	–	12%	–	L*	H
Linseed	25%	12%	–	–	L	H
Soya bean meal	45%	6%	–	–	L	H
Field beans	20%	1·2%	4·1%	–	L	H
Liquid molasses	14%	1·75%	–	37·8%	–	–
Molasses meal	14%	–	5·5%	38%	–	–
Sugar beet pulp	18%	–	15%	22%	–	–
Milk pellets	23%	15·5%	–	–	Vit/min	–
Skim milk powder	23%	17%	–	–	Vit/min	–
Carrots	15%	–	8%			
Potatoes	15%	–	8%			
Grass meal	10%	4%	10%	–	–	–
Horse and pony nuts	10%	2·5%	15%	–	Vit/min	added
Racehorse nuts	14%	3·5%	9%	–	Vit/min	added
Complete nuts	10%	2·5%	20%	–	Vit/min	added
Stud nuts	15%	3·5%	6%	–	Vit/min	added
Horse concentrate pellets	26%	3%	8·5%	–	Vit/min	added
Horse and pony 'mix'	11%	3%	7%	–	Vit/min	added

In order to achieve a balanced ration – sufficient starch for energy produced by cereal foods and protein – boosted by the inclusion of high protein foods in small quantities, we must decide which of the foregoing feeds we wish to use for a particular horse. Though starch will produce energy and warmth, the horse must have protein at the correct percentage to prevent damage to its whole make-up – muscles, blood, bones. They all will fail, unless there is enough protein present backed up by vitamins and minerals to ensure that the horse is capable of carrying out the task required of it.

Horses in light work (children's ponies and horses being used for quiet riding for about an hour a day) require approximately 10 per cent protein; those in medium work (bigger ponies and horses going for a decent ride with cantering and jumping) come into the 12 per cent protein bracket, while those really being asked to work (either at fast paces over a concentrated or extended period of time) such as racehorses, eventers, hunters, long distance horses must have at least 14 per cent protein, and may need slightly more in some cases depending on their rider's capabilities. You must feed not only for the work, but also with the rider's ability in mind; if very careful you can match the two, otherwise should a horse prove too much for the rider concerned, then rather than deprive the horse of the correct food the rider must be changed for one capable of controlling that horse, when correctly fed.

Breeding and youngstock require even higher protein for their needs together with additional calcium – 15 per cent protein is the figure to aim at here. Whereas, with cereals like oats and the lower percentage protein horse nuts, one has to feed a fairly large amount by weight to achieve the feeding value required, it is the reverse (with very limited amounts) with high protein foods like milk pellets – high in protein but not heating. So they are suitable for inclusion in diets where the protein must be raised but the horse or pony must remain sober.

Soya bean meal – very high protein and, being a bean, heating, is unsuitable for ordinary horses and ponies except breeding and youngstock or horses in very hard work.

Horse beans because they are high in energy and protein, are therefore only for those in hard work with an experienced rider on board.

Linseed is one of the best sources of additional protein as it has many advantages and does not tend to make a horse hot up. In addition soya bean meal has one other added advantage as a balancer, it is one of the few foods available that is high in amino-acids – the essential ones like lysine, which is very low in oats and similar foods; so by including soya bean meal in a diet the amino-acid balance is restored to a certain extent, thereby helping the growth rate of youngstock.

In the old days it was safe to feed cattle rearing pencils (nuts), but nowadays the inclusion of such items as urea and hormones in many cattle feeds, render it very unwise as they are not safe for horses.

An imbalance in diet or incorrect feeding – too much or too little will lead to trouble sooner or later. In most cases it will be sooner, so feed carefully and feed wisely; and if in any doubt call your veterinary surgeon without delay.

We come finally now to see how best we can achieve our object of a sound, healthy horse that is fit and ready to carry out anything we ask of it. Having studied our particular horse and made a note of its size, type, age, present condition (is it soft off grass, or has it been receiving a concentrate ration, and what are we really expecting from the horse?) we can start to work out a suitable feed chart for that given horse.

I do not propose to deal with stable management, exercise or anything other than feeding is this book – my other books *Horse By Horse* and *Getting Your Horse Fit* cover those subjects fully.

Feeding Chart

Whatever your horse you will require a feeding chart for it, not only for your own daily reference, but for those whose job it might be to feed in your absence.

Having decided the overall amount of food your horse requires, then divide it up into roughage and concentrates, remembering to match food to work, and work to food. The more work required of a horse the greater the amount of concentrates it will require in comparison to the roughage – as you increase one, decrease the other so as to always equal the same overall amount; in the same way if you decrease the work, then decrease the concentrates and increase the roughage.

It is all a matter of commonsense and not really all that complicated. How diets can vary according to the different role in life a horse can lead, can be seen from two of Galavant's feeding charts – the first (Figure 10.1) was for the spring of 1975, her last year eventing following a very good season's hunting, and the other (Figure 10.2) was the winter of 1978 for her and River Gipsy (who remained together as the foal was born so late and we felt she would benefit from the extra time with her dam, who was not in foal again).

Figure 10.1   GALAVANT Spring Eventing

Breakfast
6.15 am   ½lb (227 g) bran
                   1 lb (454 g) oats (bruised)
                   ½lb (227 g) nuts
                   ¼ flaked maize
                   4 handfuls choppy
                   1 measure (½oz) (14·18 g) ground limestone
                   1 measure Equivite milk pellets (4 0z) (113 g)
                   (We had been giving Equivite supplement, but changed to
                     give added protein for eventing.)
                   ½oz (14·18 g) salt (1 des.sp.)
                   Mix with 1 teasp. black treacle in ½pt (250 cc) warm water

6 lb (2·7 kg) hay net after morning exercise.

Lunch
12.30 pm   ½lb (227 g) bran
                   1½lb (680 g) oats
                   ½lb (227 g) nuts
                   4 handfuls choppy
                   1 measure Equivite milk pellets (4oz) (113 g)
                   Mix with black treacle (1 teasp.) in ½pt (250 cc) warm water

Tea
5 pm   ½lb (227 g) bran
                   1½lb (680 g) oats
                   1 lb (454 g) nuts
                   ¼lb (113 g) flaked maize
                   4 handfuls choppy
                   1 measure ground limestone
                   1½ measures Equivite milk pellets (6oz) (170 g)
                   1 des.sp. salt (½oz) (14·18 g)
                   Mix as above; or with linseed, in which case leave out black
                     treacle

8 lb (3·6 kg) hay net at night

Supper, Mash Night: Linseed mash once a week or after hunting or
    competition – followed by rest next rest day. Cut oats by 1 lb (454 g),
    remainder of feeds the same as walked out for ½ hr.
Exercise 1–3 hrs Rug when cold. ½ hr grazing walk rest days.
Rugs: Rug and blanket all the time; top door shut dusk open morning stables.

So much for the feeding chart when in hard work, now for a look at one for the same mare but when she was feeding a growing foal, who was sharing the same food in addition to the milk she was still receiving.

Figure 10.2   GALAVANT AND RIVER GIPSY January (Mare and foal 6 months)

Breakfast
6.15 am
        ¾ lb (340 g) bran
        2½ lb (1·1 kg) oats
        ¼ lb (113 g) flaked maize
        ¼ lb (113 g) soya bean meal
        2 handfuls choppy
        2 measures Equivite supplement
        1 measure ground limestone
        1 dsp. salt
        1 tsp. black treacle mixed in ½ pt (250 cc) of warm water to damp feed

Lunch
12.45 pm
        ¾ lb (340 g) bran
        2½ lb (1·1 kg) oats
        ¼ lb (113 g) flaked maize
        ¼ lb (113 g) soya bean meal
        2 measures Equivite supplement
        1 tsp. black treacle in warm water as before
        Sliced carrots if available

Tea
4.45 pm
        ¾ lb (340 g) bran
        2½ lb (1·1 kg) oats
        ¼ lb (113 g) flaked maize
        ¼ lb (113 g) soya bean meal
        2 handfuls choppy
        2 measures Equivite supplement
        1 measure ground limestone
        1 dsp. salt
        1 tsp. black treacle in water to mix; or cooked linseed (6 oz) (170 g) before soaking and cooking; 2 nights a week in place of treacle

Cod liver oil was added to this diet about the middle of February at the rate of ½ oz (14·18 g) (half a wineglass full) morning and evening.

Hay: About 28 to 30 lb (12 to 13 kg) of best mixture divided into 5–6 feeds a day, with the breakfast, midday and evening feeds the largest and additional hay given in the field, during their time out every morning, during the afternoon and again at 9 pm. This was to try and give as near natural feeding as possible – a little and often to avoid waste and help digestion. Extra work, but worth it.

Top door: Shut at night and open morning stables.

These are just two charts, there are many other variations, but remember to make all changes slowly over several days; do not use more than one brand of supplement at a time, though providing there is no cod liver oil in your supplement, this and a calcium balancer like ground limestone can be added on veterinary advice if required. It is foolhardy to go experimenting on your own account unless you are dead sure you are correct – your fit horse will be a sick horse!

Now we will examine the different diets required for the many roles in life our horses play, each one necessitating something different.

Broodmares and Foals

Basically a mare will require the same overall food as if she was in work – that is a 16hh mare of Thoroughbred type would require $27\frac{1}{2}$lb (12·47kg) of food per day. Initially she can be fed normally on a working diet, but for the last third of her pregnancy she will require additional protein, to raise her diet to 15 per cent protein, and increased calcium to meet the needs of the growing foetus which will, during the final months, be making an ever-increasing demand on the mare's own system. As time goes on and the mare gets larger the bulk food must be decreased and the high protein concentrate ration increased (if nuts are used they should be stud nuts). Aim at a ratio of 40 per cent roughage – 60 per cent concentrates – as the room within is diminishing, so do not over-load the digestive system at any one feed. Rather, give more feeds and avoid at all cost anything that could cause colic or upsets. Spring grass – high in natural protein will replace much of the hay for April to June foalers, others will require high protein concentrates. Exercise is essential, if necessary give inhand exercise until the mare is too heavy, then leave at grass to exercise.

After foaling the mare will require a light diet for a day or so, and then she can be gradually put back onto her full concentrate ration, but remember she is now feeding a foal. This will mean one, she has to nourish herself and, two, provide an ever-increasing supply of rich milk for that foal. As the foal will very soon, given the opportunity, investigate the mare's supply of concentrates, care must be taken to ensure that the food is suitable for a very small foal and easily digested as, within a week, the foal will be eating too. This is where milk pellets are such a help – a rich source of protein of the easily digested variety, backed up by a full range of carefully balanced vitamins and minerals. In fact a foal can start having a few milk pellets out of your hand at three-days-old. Weakness can only be overcome by correct feeding – the mare's milk, if of the correct quality, is the foal's basic source of nourishment, but very often the milk is not of the quality needed and an additional source of food is vitally necessary if the foal is to grow up strong and healthy.

Once a foal is eating, not only grass (which if of good quality will provide easily digested nourishment) but hard food too, half the battle is over. By four-weeks-old River Gipsy was eating her share of the rations, which consisted of bran, oats, and milk pellets mixed with two handfuls of choppy (the choppy was kept low in order to ensure that River Gipsy got the maximum amount of nourishment from the amount of food she could consume) and damped with black treacle and warm water. On top of this both Galavant and River Gipsy had their ground limestone and a small dose of Equivite supplement; while out in the field, to play with, I placed a 'Rockie'. Hay was provided in the loose box and as the grass grew short, in the field too. It paid off – River Gipsy's legs were beginning to straighten, and her joints too. By six-weeks-old, she was looking a different foal.

Some foals are born strong and active, getting to their feet within a short space of time and diving in to start sucking with vigour; others are not so strong. With extreme care these foals can be saved and grow up to be normal – problems have a habit of sorting themselves out given time and understanding.

River Gipsy had a difficult arrival and required veterinary assistance – small, with exceptionally long legs, the tendons of which were shorter than the bones, she was able to stand and totter about. At birth she was 37 inches (93·98cm). Conformation and colour-wise she was all I wished for, it was her legs that were the problem, and the fact that she could not suck. Galavant, sensing all was not well, rejected her – this is common with animals in the circumstances and must be overcome. What is vital for all new-born foals is the colostrum – the first milk which contains 20 per cent or more protein and is higher in fat than the later milk and is normally rich in vitamins A and D, providing the mare has had these in her food. Acting like a natural purgative for the young animal, it clears all the accumulated faecal matter, meconium, from the intestine. This meconium is often dry and putty-like in consistency, and if a foal does not pass it within a few hours of birth it will die. Watch out, therefore, for the passing of this black like substance, and once the droppings turn yellow you will know that the foal is getting its milk. This colostrum also supplies the foal with its first antibodies to protect it against various bacteria and viruses.

Our problem was to get River Gipsy to suck and persuade Galavant to accept her so that she could. I tried on my own and with help, neither succeeded; in the end only one answer remained – Galavant had to be milked off and the foal bottle fed. Easier said than done; I had milked cows, but a mare who resented being touched was another matter! Using forefinger and thumb, I managed to gently milk off nearly half a pint into a sterilised glass jug; this was then poured into a glass bottle (sterilised) and a calf teat (sterilised) placed on top. Gently I cradled the foal's tiny head in my arm and raised her head into a sucking position, as near nature's position as possible, and placed the teat between her lips alongside her tongue. Little by little, a drop at a time I let the milk run into her mouth, stopping every second or two to let her rest and swallow; after about five minutes she had taken a couple of ounces and I let her rest.

As the sun was shining and she was cold and breathing badly, we carried her outside and laid her in the sun to warm through, and, I hoped, get to her feet. This she did, while I thoroughly mucked out the box and filled it up with a very deep bed of clean straw. Back in the box two hours later, we fed her again. Every hour or two I repeated the tiny feeds, warming the milk to blood heat by standing the bottle in water – possibly not the best of ideas but it was impossible to milk Galavant single-handed and I had no more help till 5 p.m. and had to cope on my own. About 4 p.m. River Gipsy started to give faint sucks for herself and there was some hope, her head and neck were bending more easily into the correct position to reach Galavant once the mare would accept her. Before each bottle feed I tried to persuade the foal to suck from her dam, and also to try and encourage Galavant to accept her daughter. At 5 p.m. our neighbour's cowman returned to help again and between us we restrained Galavant so that I could milk her out – not only did I require the milk for River Gipsy's feeds through the night, but unless I eased the pressure on Galavant's udder she was not going to allow the foal to suck. Just as I was finishing, a minute muzzle was pushed in over my arm – River Gipsy had come of her own accord and in no time was sucking away in ecstasy, the old mare slowly relaxed and let down more milk. At long last the foal had had a full feed – we had hope.

During the afternoon after one of her bottle feeds, River Gipsy had passed the meconium, so at least her inside was working, and now, after her full feed, it worked again and this time the droppings were of the correct yellow colour for a milk-fed animal. Unless she started to scour, we had cleared the first major hurdle. If a foal starts to scour you must send for help without delay, it could be very serious; we were fortunate and River Gipsy never suffered in this way, in fact she hardly did so when Galavant was due on at her foal heat; foals will scour then, but it should not persist, if it does call help. Never be too proud to ask your veterinary surgeon for advice and help. For one thing, should a virus be going round, they will know about it (you probably won't) and time could be all-important.

I went on offering bottles to River Gipsy throughout the evening and, at 2 a.m., the following morning she pushed aside the bottle and went direct to her fresh supply with Galavant doing more than shift her weight, so that she could adjust her hind leg to let the little filly feed in peace – we had made it. I knew now River Gipsy would be safe with the mare, and the mare in her turn would settle down to her role as broodmare.

I have told River Gipsy's story in the hope that it will help others faced with a task of this kind, to fight for their foal's life and not just let things take their own course – a dead foal is no foal, only a bitter disappointment. As for River Gipsy her legs took ten months to straighten and strengthen; many only take a matter of weeks. There is no set time, and only careful feeding can help matters along on a satisfactory course.

As the weeks pass the combined ration for mare and foal require increasing, as the foal will be taking more for itself. To start with a foal will only eat a handful or two at each feed, then by the time it is a few weeks old it will be eating quite a little meal in addition to grass and hay. If born about April, with the flush of grass, then mare and foal will not require so much extra feeding; in fact in good years the grass may be sufficient to provide all the protein required. Whereas you must not under-feed, you must not over-feed either.

From about three months onwards watch out for the foal's joints swelling as this means inflammation has set in affecting the growing ends of the bones, which in early life are still soft. At the first signs consult your veterinary surgeon, for the causes could be feeding or a deficiency, and righting matters will require professional help.

Periostitis – inflammation of the surfaces of the bones, is another condition requiring expert help if the horse is not to become permanently lame; if caught in time, then it can be cured fairly quickly with the correct treatment.

Teeth in a young foal, and all during its growing life, are a special consideration – bad teeth leads to bad feeding. Keep an eye on how the teeth are being cut and if they are coming through correctly.

At about two-months-old the foal will be able to cope with a more varied diet, and can gradually be weaned off the milk pellets (unless you can afford to go on buying them) and introduced to soya bean meal and flaked maize in readiness for its first winter. Soya bean meal at 45 per cent protein is excellent for producing growth and the flaked maize will provide the starch content, for energy. Fed in conjunction with oats, a vitamin/mineral supplement, and additional calcium the foal should be getting a diet to encourage it to grow and mature. But remember this is a very rich diet and must not be over-fed, or the foal will become very hard to control when being led. One can control them, but must realise that the foal is very 'corned up' and not take any stupid liberties with it. I would far rather teach a foal to behave under these conditions than have it so meek that it did nothing until it came to be broken and tasted food of any quality for the first time. Cod liver oil may be desirable in addition to the above, but ask first before making the diet too rich, for then you could have trouble of another kind on your hands. The usual ratio for this type of ration is 20 per cent bran; 60 per cent oats; 10 per cent flaked maize and 10 per cent high protein food (soya bean meal or milk pellets).

The latter group should not exceed 1 lb (0·45 kg) per day, and it is wise to under-feed this amount for foals from smaller mares – that is under 16 hh, until you see how they can take it. Milk pellets are safe at the recommended amounts, it is such foods as the soya bean meal one has to be so careful not to over-feed. A foal will require about 1 lb (0·45 kg) of food of the above mixture or stud nuts. If these are fed in place of a mixed feed, for every month of its life up to a maximum of 8 lb (3·62 kg) per day.

In order to regulate Galavant's and River Gipsy's ration I stopped increasing the total amount when Galavant's own requirements started to decline with the decrease in her milk after four months. River Gipsy merely took more and therefore the mare got less until they were level pegging. Many people feed foals out of separate bowls. I have always fed mine along with the mare either out of the manger – which incidently must have the corner feeder bars removed for safety's sake – or, if outside, in a manger on the fence. This, after a while, will get too small for two faces, then a feed tin or nylon bowl which will take two heads with comfort, will be required. If you have more than one mare and foal in a field, or two separate horses, then the bowls must be well apart to stop fighting.

Orphan Foals

Orphan foals are those that have either lost their dams at birth, or been abandoned within a week or two of birth. They require special treatment and care, so it is far safer to seek professional advice than rely on books.

But remember two things: first, absolute cleanliness; second, feeding will be required every two hours without fail until the foal is at least six-weeks-old, then the feeds can be spaced out a little more if you are going to rear a healthy foal.

Weanlings

All foals, once they are weaned and before they have reached their second winter, are weanlings. Before weaning ensure that the foal can eat and drink properly and is well used to hard food and hay. To wean before the foal has become used to these foods is cruel. Foals can be weaned at four months, but it is far wiser to run them on to five or six months if possible, the longer they have their dam's milk the better for them. Only if the mare is in foal again or cannot cope, should they be weaned.

Some people wean early if the foal gets too playful; true, they may get rather a handful, but this is no excuse to wean them. Six months is the ideal age. The foal must be housed warmly at night and given three feeds a day – two in the box and one out in the paddock if out all day. Shelter is required if you are going to leave young foals out in all weathers, otherwise put them out for 2 to 4 hours and bring them back in to a dry bed and more hay. A companion is necessary to prevent unhappiness.

Foals can be yarded all the time, but exercise is essential and, if at all possible, all youngstock should be put out for an hour or so everyday, even in snow, otherwise their high protein diet will become too much for them. Owing to their rapid rate of growth (80 per cent of their ultimate height in the first year) foals must have adequate protein (15 per cent) and calcium, backed by other vitamins and minerals in some form or other, to satisfy the demands being made upon their systems. Deprive a foal of this nourishment in the first year and the ground lost can never be regained. The overall amount of food depends on their mature height and size. Feed accordingly, but do not give more than 8 lb (3·62 kg) of concentrates per day, and use only the very best quality food.

Youngstock

During the spring of the year following the foal's birth, its concentrate ration will be reduced as the spring grass, rich in natural protein, gradually replaces the high protein cereal diet it has been having during the winter.

Once the weather is warm enough and there is a plentiful supply of grass, the foal can be turned out with others for company to enjoy the summer and grow on in peace. The following winter the foal, now a yearling, will require the same quality food as the previous winter, for now it is filling out and building up its body structure, but the quantity of concentrates will be about two-thirds that of the previous winter, unless it is thought advisable to give more. Use your commonsense and, if in doubt, seek advice. These first three years are vital to the youngster's future.

Some people give no concentrates during the third winter, but youngstock require to be kept warm and for this they require energy food. Small ponies maybe, can now do without, but horses who mature later and go on growing often till they are five, require concentrates, given in two or three feeds a day with all the best hay then can eat, plus of course their vitamins/ minerals and additional calcium. Stint them young and they will be stunted for life and when asked to work, will be unable to withstand the strain.

Showing

Both in hand, or under saddle, showing requires the horse to be in such condition that it is carrying more flesh than would be normal if allowed to either grow on at its own pace, or was in hard work. Youngstock tend to get 'over-topped' – too fat – for they cannot get enough exercise and this, in turn, accompanied by long hours in a horse box on the roads and endless walking on hard ground in the show ring, tends to give rise to leg troubles.

So, if you wish your young horse to work hard in later life, by all means show, but take care not to over-do the fattening foods required to make them into 'big' condition, it is just not worth it. Fashion, when followed slavishly, is a dangerous thing and a great deal of harm can arise. Mature horses shown under saddle suffer in the same way, but their bones are set and so it is jarring and their wind that ultimately cause trouble. Use moderation in all things and success, if your stock is good enough, will follow; make your horse fit – not fat.

Transit

Travelling calls for special feeding because the horse is standing for long hours. If not being called upon to compete or work hard once arrived at its destination, the horse will benefit from a hay net to pull at during the journey. It helps them relax, and prevents them from going long hours without food.

If they are competing, then feed in the normal way before leaving, giving the nervous ones sufficient time to digest their meal before being loaded. Competition horses require to be without food, and water, for at least two hours to allow for complete digestion before undertaking hard work. So adjust your feeding according to work. Take a feed along in a portable manger or feed tin, also a supply of fresh drinking water, a flask of boiling water to remove chill from drinking water if required, and a full hay net for the return journey.

On arrival back home, or at the end of a long journey moving a horse from A to B, give only a hay net and a light supper of a bran, or linseed mash, as the horse will be very tired and cannot digest a heavy concentrate feed. Once rested, they can be given a small feed of concentrates, if so wished. Horses having undertaken very long journeys will require several days to recover – horses coming from abroad, especially Ireland by boat, suffer a lot if not properly cared for. My first horse, Witchery, a grey six-year-old mare came from Ireland. We discovered she had only been broken for two weeks, having been made to pull a plough in Ireland as part of her breaking, before being backed and shipped over to Cambridge Horse Sales. From there she came by train to our home on the Essex coast, where we kept her at a neighbouring farm. We had been warned not to give her any corn, only hay, which we did – what we omitted to do in our ignorance was to give her a bran mash. In consequence, we found ourselves with a sick horse and case of colic on our hands. I had learnt my first real lesson in horsemastership, and the vast difference between riding other people's horses and caring for one's own! So, if you do travel your horse, take care of it and do not just push it into a box or out into a field, and leave it. If the journey has been long and they are really tired they require warmth and easily digested food for the first 24 hours.

Sickness

Sickness will strike every stable sooner or later, and in most cases sooner. A sick horse requires keeping to as normal a routine as possible, though if confined to its box, must have its concentrates reduced or eliminated altogether, depending on veterinary advice. Replace them with 'false' feeds as already described, and if the horse is reluctant to eat, they must be coaxed and encouraged by extra tempting feeds. Their strength must be kept up or they will never recover.

Hand feeding is one of the best ways, a little at a time. I have spent hours crouched in the corner of a box with a sick horse, just offering a handful every five minutes – it is surprising how much over 24 hours you can get into them. Oddly enough if you settle down with them in a box, providing they are quiet and will not kick you, your very presence will encourage them.

If the horse is suffering from a throat or wind complaint and requires damped hay there are three ways of achieving this, two I do not favour much, the third I always employ.

(1) Play a cold water hose over a full net of well shaken up hay, until it is thoroughly soaked, then hang up to drain – the best of the cold methods as germs cannot be passed on.

(2) Immerse the whole net in a tank of water and leave to soak. Not to be encouraged unless a special tank is kept for each horse and the water changed every time a net is soaked. Nets carry infection and if soaked in a communal water tank will certainly spread disease; and should anyone be so foolish as to then use the water from that tank for the horses' drinking water – even if the horses were deemed healthy, and were only having their nets soaked against wind trouble – they should stop and think just what they are doing. Such water is quite unfit for horses to drink, and if trouble ensues it is entirely the owner's fault.

(3) Using boiling water, take a full net of well shaken hay and place it on the ground, on a clean spot – pour the kettle of boiling water over the net, turning the net as you do so in order to get the net thoroughly damp and water running right through. Once wet, hang up to drain and cool; this will take about half an hour and, before feeding, plunge your hand into the very centre of the net to ensure there are no hot spots to burn the horse. Hay damped in this way does not go soggy and slimy, and retains its palatability – in fact it is partly steamed. The boiling water tends to disinfect the net and as it is no longer boiling when it reaches the inside of the net, only on the outer edge, the vitamin content should not be too much affected. Heat can destroy vitamins, but it must be a steady heat over a given time – like boiling in a saucepan of water over a fire. Remember when dealing with sick horses, cleanliness (clean all bowls, buckets etc., carefully

after each feed and use separate ones for each horse) and quietness are essential to recovery.

Resting

Every horse requires a rest or a holiday for part of the year. If given in summer, than all they should require while the grass has nourishment in it, is good grazing, water and shelter to provide shade and protection should they require it. But do ensure that in hot weather they are coming out of their shade to drink, otherwise they will get dehydrated. In winter, every horse regardless of size and type requires extra feeding for maintenance. Small ponies will manage on hay and possibly a feed of concentrates in hard weather to maintain their body heat.

Really bad weather will require two feeds a day and all the hay the horses can eat. But be careful: ponies, even in winter, can go down with laminitis, especially in wet conditions when many stand around until the blood fails to circulate in their legs and feet. The blood runs down all right, but must be pumped back up again by means of the action of the frog on the ground; failure to move about means the blood merely stagnates causing fever-in-the-feet, to give laminitis its other name.

Horses will require feeding with concentrates in addition to hay, otherwise they suffer. Better to bring horses in at night to be fed and sleep dry, and turn out by day. Feed out of mangers well spaced out on the fence, or in feed tins well apart if horses are out together. Their food can be of the 10 per cent protein type if mature.

Pet ponies that only work very lightly – leading rein ponies and ones used for quiet rides once or twice a week for a short time, can be treated as if resting.

Working

We now come to the section where we have to decide what category of work our horse comes under. Those in light work – an hour's hacking once a day or at weekends – require a 10 per cent protein diet of about 5 to 6 lb (2·26 to 2·72 kg) for a 15·2 hh to 16 hh horse. The same amount, or possibly slightly more if doing medium work, 1 hour's moderately active schooling, jumping, cantering, or just a good active hack – but of 12 per cent protein. Horses really working hard – competition work, hunting, long exercise in between work sessions or competitions – require 14 per cent protein and the horse will require 10 to 14 lb (4·53 to 6·35 kg) per day of this high protein diet, but must be fed according to the work done. If work is cut for some reason, then so too must be the intake of food. Hay makes up the difference in these rations. Racehorses will require even more possibly, as will three-day eventers, but then they are burning up their energy by work. Remember, all horses stabled and in work will require keeping warm, no horse can make the most of its food if it is cold in its stable. Some horses in the lighter categories of work can run out each day for an hour or two, and will benefit from the relaxation and chance to pick some grass, even if the nourishment in winter is negligible. In the summer the two can be mixed with great advantage for all but those in really hard work, and even these gain from a chance to eat some grass each day.

Before going further a look at a progressive feeding chart will give you a chance to see how to build up your horse's food slowly over a period of time to match work to food.

A horse of 16 hh can start at 5 lb (2·26 kg) of concentrates a day, having worked up gradually to that amount over the previous week. A small horse will start at less, 2 lb (0·90 kg) and stop increasing sooner; 7 to 10 lb (3·17 to 4·53 kg) for a 15 hh horse in hard work starting at ½ lb (0·22 kg) and working up, but do not exceed about 4 lb (1·81 kg) of concentrates for a 14 hh pony – less for a smaller one; but ponies can follow the same routine if they are going to work, but *small* ponies must never have high protein food once mature and being ridden by children. They should have a low protein diet, horse and pony nuts being a suitable feed at 10 per cent, as oats are normally too heating and excitable-making for small ponies and inexperienced children.

Once the child can ride fairly well and they have a bigger pony, then this pony can be fed concentrates to match its work. do not give the high protein type to ponies as it is not their nature to have rich food – the hill ponies show us the type of land they thrive on when grazing is plentiful; feed well, but feed wisely. Milk pellets are about the only exception from the high

Figure 10.3 PROGRESSIVE FEEDING CHART

Week	1	2	3	4	5	6	7	8	9	10	11	12
Hay (including Choppy)	22½	21½	20½	19½	17	16	15	14	13	12	11	10
Concentrate Ration	5	6	7	8	9	10	11	12	13	14	15	16
Bran	1½	1½	1½	1½	2	2	2	2	2	2	2	2
Total	28	28	28	28	28	28	28	28	28	28	28	28
No. Feeds	3	3	3	3	4	4	4	4	4	4	4	4 (only for those in very hard work)

protein range – the protein here being derived from milk is not heating or excitable-making, therefore the makers claim it is safe, and I have certainly found milk pellets invaluable in diets where the temperament of horse and rider have to be matched and at the same time provide extra protein. Driving horses and ponies require feeding in exactly the same way as if they were going to be ridden. Adjusting their food to match their work and the size and ability of their driver.

The process is gradual and various feeding stuffs need to be chosen with care bearing in mind that the roughage/concentrate ration must never fall below 40 per cent roughage and 60 per cent concentrates, even for horses in hard work. For those in normal work 60 to 40 per cent would be in order, or possibly 50 to 50 per cent; then there is no reason why your horse should not be fit and contented and capable of undertaking whatever work is required of it.

Old Horses

Horses in their teens will start requiring more protein in their diet and additional calcium to meet the demands of their bodies in the natural run down of increasing years, so slowly start to revert to the type of diet for youngstock.

Well reared and fed throughout their formative and working lives, horses should have a life span into their twenties or beyond. Our old Jackie was well over 40 years when, sadly, he had to be put down when our farm was sold. Still fit and well, he had come with the farm some five years before unable to eat, and the previous owners had stated he required no shelter or extra food! His teeth merely required serious attention – once done he never looked back. Horses teeth must have attention twice a year, and they must have food that they can easily digest and is of a highly nourishing nature. True care and warmth means many extra years if sound – if unsound, then it is cruel to keep them. Horses over twelve years require an annual check up for heart, wind and eyes, besides teeth – and if fit can go on working providing they get the required warmth and nourishment to combat old age.

In conclusion I hope this book has helped to answer many of the questions concerning feeding so as to enable readers to enjoy the benefits that come from a fit horse whose coat shines and muscles ripple beneath a soft, supple skin.

Nevertheless, do not throw all your hard work away by inadvertently letting your horse have access to any chocolate before or during any sport or competition subject to routine dope testing. Theobromine-Caffeine is a stimulant and therefore forbidden. Keep Mars bars well out of the way and even Polos, are best kept for when no competitions are at stake, though at present they have not caused problems, that anyone knows of. But formulas can change and then it would be too late.

CONVERSION TABLE KILOGRAMMES TO POUNDS
(Kg – lbs – Kg)
© Diana R. Tuke

KG	LB	KG
50	110 (1 cwt = 112 lb)	50
45	99·0	45
40	88·0	40
35	77·0	35
30	66·0	30
25	55·0 (½ cwt = 56 lb)	25
20	44·0	20
15	33·0	15
14	30.8	14
13	28·6 (¼ cwt = 28 lb)	13
12	26·4	12
11	24·2	11
10	22·0	10
9	19·8	9
8	17·5	8
7	15·4	7
	(1 stone = 15 lb)	
3	13·2	6
	11·0	5
4	8·8	4
	6·6	3
	4·4	2
	2·2	1
½ (g)	1·1 (1 lb = 454 g)	½
¼ (2 g)	0·55 (½ lb = 8 oz = 227 g)	¼
⅛ (g)	0·275 (¼ lb = 4 oz = 113 g)	⅛
	(3 oz = 82·125 g)	
(oz)	0·1375 (2 oz = 56·75 g)	1/16
1/32 (31·2)	0·06875 (1 oz = 28·375 g)	1/32
1/64 (15·625)	0·034375 (½ oz = 14·1875 g)	1/64

All figures are approximate

By the same author

A Long Road to Harringay
Bit by Bit
Stitch by Stitch
Horse by Horse
Getting Your Horse Fit
Rider's Handbook
Clipping Your Horse